P9-CNH-609

THE BIRTH OF THE REPUBLIC, 1763–89

The
Birth of the Republic
1763–89
Revised Edition

Edmund S. Morgan

CHICAGO HISTORY OF AMERICAN CIVILIZATION
Daniel J. Boorstin, EDITOR

THE UNIVERSITY OF CHICAGO PRESS
Chicago and London

The University of Chicago Press, Chicago 60637
The University of Chicago Press, Ltd., London

© 1956, 1977 by the University of Chicago. All rights
reserved. Published 1956. Revised edition 1977
Printed in the United States of America

90 89   9 8 7

ISBN: 0-226-53758-7 (clothbound); 0-226-53759-5 (paperbound)
Library of Congress Catalog Card Number: 77-70169

FOR HELEN

Contents

vii

Editor's Preface

During the past two decades, this book has proven to be one of the most popoular and most persuasive scholarly accounts of the American Revolution. The continuing appeal of Professor Morgan's book is doubly impressive, for these twenty years, climaxing in the Bicentennial celebration, have brought numerous books of enduring scholarly value, and still more numerous by-products of popular or academic fads. Now Professor Morgan has sifted all these and drawn on his own extensive research, to make this revision.

In this new edition, Professor Morgan preserves the unity which has helped give this book its reputation and its influence. His vigorous thesis is that belief in principle and the search for principle can shape history and did shape the founding of the nation. He enriches his account with vivid everyday detail and rewards us with a suspense story. How would these diverse scattered colonists be able to defeat what was then the most powerful nation on earth? How could they manage to draw themselves together in a durable constitution, to create a republic that would occupy a continent?

He has made this a convincing suspense story because he knows the setting of the story so well, and he strengthens its scholarly persuasiveness by taking account of the most recent work of other scholars. While some others have been tempted to make the story an exercise in a particular overemphasis, he has resisted the temptation.

Editor's Preface

Just as the story told in this book is in the mainstream of our national history, so Professor Morgan's interpretation puts him in the mainstream of American historical writing. Readers can here sample the wide vision, the scholarly scrupulousness, and the literary grace which have kept alive the writings of our best American historians. These qualities have made their writing itself a historic force in the building, the humanizing, and the strengthening of our nation.

This volume will introduce the reader to the Chicago History of American Civilization. The series offers lively and readable scholarly books on all aspects of our history. The "chronological" group, of which this is one, provides a coherent narrative of our whole national career. The "topical" group offers histories of many aspects of American civilization—philanthropy, religion, railroads, folklore, labor, music, among others. The series still grows, and new volumes are added from time to time.

DANIEL J. BOORSTIN

Preface to the Revised Edition

In the twenty years since the first edition of this book appeared, historians studying the American Revolution have turned up so many new facts and suggested so many new interpretations of familiar facts that it seemed high time to make revisions and additions to this survey of the subject. The theme of the book remains as it was, the search by Americans of the Revolutionary period for principles on which they could take a common stand. The discovery of their willingness to coalesce around the principle of human equality still seems to me the most exciting thing about the Revolution. I hope that, from the work of other scholars as well as from my own continuing studies, I have achieved a richer understanding of how it happened. And I hope that the resulting changes in the text will enhance whatever contribution it may make to those who read it. To that end I have also added an Appendix containing the basic documents in which the Revolutionists embodied the ideas that brought them together.

September 1976   E.S.M.

Lexington Green

The men had been waiting since a little after midnight. Revere arrived about that time with his warning, and they tumbled out of bed and gathered on the common, where they shivered in the cold, clear April night for an hour or more. Now some had gone home and the rest were in the tavern, waiting nervously as candles flickered lower, for the roll of drums that would call them out again.

No one was quite sure what they were supposed to do. No word had come from Concord or Boston to tell them. They must assemble. They must be ready. But for what? It was not suggested that they dispute the passage of the royal troops to Concord. No, they would simply stand there on the common, drawn up in military array, displaying by their formal presence the invincible dislike of Americans for what the British were up to.

By the time the first streaks of dawn appeared, it began to seem that nothing was going to happen after all. It was several hours since Revere brought his message and still no sign of the force he described. There must have been that tinge of disappointment we all feel despite our relief when some expected and exciting danger fails to materialize. Then Thaddeus Bowman was galloping up. They were coming! They were almost here! Grabbing of muskets, roll of drums, shouts of alarm, and Captain John Parker leads seventy men to the green in time to see the first columns of redcoats swing into view.

There is no need for the British to cross the green. The road to Concord runs along the left side of it, and Captain Parker has no intention of putting his men on that road. He will keep them on the green where they will be visible, perhaps audible, but out of the British line of march. Suddenly a British officer, in the uniform of a major of marines, is cantering across the grass, calling upon him and his men to disperse and lay down their arms. The regulars have broken into a run; they are pouring onto the green, cheering wildly as they come. Parker, alarmed, gives the order to disperse, and the Americans, who have scarcely formed ranks yet, start to fall back, a few standing fast, refusing to budge. On both sides the men are out of control, and before anyone knows what has happened firing begins.

Pitcairn, the major of marines, signals frantically but vainly to stop it. The Americans, vastly outnumbered and already scattering, are driven from the field, leaving eight dead and ten wounded. The British officers, disgruntled and embarrassed, recover control, allow their men a formal cheer, and then hurry them on toward Concord.

Thus inauspiciously began the war which produced the United States. One can scarcely imagine a more confused or futile gesture than that of the militiamen who stood on Lexington Green on that nineteenth of April in 1775. But we will make a bad mistake if we take their confusion to be a sign of irresolution or uncertainty or even of mere foolishness. No war had begun when they hurried out of the tavern to take their places on the green. They did not think they were rushing into battle but simply into a posture of righteousness.

Lexington, in fact, was not really a battle. It was a moment of transition between thought and action, between peace and war. For

Lexington Green

eleven years before it Americans had been thinking and talking about their rights, issuing resolutions and petitions and declarations, enunciating the principles of government that they thought would preserve their freedom. The men who stood on Lexington Green stood there to testify to those principles. When they were attacked, they may have been surprised and momentarily confused, but they did not need to be told that the time had now come to fight. In the afternoon when the troops came back from Concord, it was the Lexington men who attacked, along with militiamen from other nearby towns, and the British who showed confusion as they fled in disorder toward Boston.

The history of the American Revolution is in part the history of the years of action that followed after Lexington, but much more it is the history of the Americans' search for principles. That search brought them to Lexington and war in 1775, but it did not end there. Throughout the years of fighting it continued and finally culminated in the adoption of the federal Constitution. It was a noble search, a daring search, and by almost any standards a successful search. The ensuing pages describe some of the difficulties overcome, some of the dangers encountered, and some of the discoveries made in the course of it.

I

The Americans and the Empire

The men who undertook the search seemed to their contemporaries—and even to themselves—as unlikely a group as could be found to join in any common enterprise. The American colonists were reputed to be a quarrelsome, litigious, divisive lot of people, and historical evidence bears out this reputation. The records of the local courts in every colony are cluttered with such a host of small lawsuits that one receives from them the impression of a people who sued each other almost as regularly as they ate or slept. Their newspapers bristle with indignant letters to the editor about matters that now seem trifling. Ministers kept the presses busy with pamphlets denouncing each other's doctrines.

Within every colony there were quarrels between different sections. Eastern Connecticut despised western Connecticut. Newport, Rhode Island, was at odds with Providence, and the rest of New England looked upon the whole of Rhode Island with undisguised contempt. Western North Carolina was so irritated by eastern North Carolina that civil war broke out in 1771. Not only did the different sections of every colony quarrel with each other, but every colony engaged in perennial boundary disputes with its neighbors. Even when faced with Indian uprisings, neighboring colonies could seldom be brought to assist each other. When New York was attacked, Massachusetts found that her budget would not allow her to send aid. When Massachusetts was attacked, the New Yorkers in turn twiddled their thumbs.

So notorious was this hostility which every American seemed to feel for every other American that James Otis, one of the early leaders in the search we are about to examine, averred in 1765 that "were these colonies left to themselves tomorrow, America would be a mere shambles of blood and confusion." And an English traveler who toured the colonies in 1759 and 1760 came to precisely the same conclusion: "Were they left to themselves, there would soon be civil war from one end of the continent to the other." Twenty years later these same people united to create a government that has had a longer continuous existence than that of any other Western country except England.

How they were able to do it must always remain a source of wonder, but with the benefit of hindsight we may see that in spite of their divisions they did have much in common. For one thing they were mainly of English descent—and proud of it. There were two large exceptions: the first a wedge of Scotch-Irish and Germans in the back country from Pennsylvania southward, the second a half-million African slaves scattered throughout the colonies but with the greatest numbers on the tobacco and rice plantations of the South. The Africans were the great exception to everything that can be said about colonial Americans. Though they did much of the work, they enjoyed few of the privileges and benefits of life in America.

For the great majority of Americans who still spoke of England as "home," even though they had never been there, being English meant having a history that stretched back continuously into a golden age of Anglo-Saxon purity and freedom. The past as it existed in their minds may have borne little resemblance to what actually happened. It was a past in which freedom, born among the Anglo-Saxons, was submerged by the Norman Conquest and only gradually recovered, the final triumph occurring in the Glorious Revolution of 1688. It was more myth than reality, but the myth served to give to the forester in New Hampshire and the cattle drover in North Carolina a pride in a common heritage. Even those parts of English history that had occurred since the founding of the colonies were cheerfully appropriated, and in the ensuing years of strife with the mother country there was no repudiation of the heritage. Throughout the war and after, Americans maintained that they were preserving the true tradition of English history, a tradition that had been upset by forces of darkness and corruption in England itself.

That such a defection should have occurred came as no surprise to the colonists, because they shared a distinctly bearish view of human nature. As they were for the most part English, so they were even more overwhelmingly Protestant. Maryland was the only colony with a substantial minority of Catholics. And except for a handful of German Lutherans, the Protestants were predominantly of Calvinist origin. Among the more sophisticated, especially in the cities and large towns, it was the fashion to take a somewhat happier view of human nature than Calvin had endorsed, but even those who thought man good enough to win heaven by his own efforts seem to have been skeptical about the likelihood of kings and statesmen making the grade. It was an outright infidel, Thomas Paine, who declared that government, like dress, is the badge of lost innocence. This common assumption, that men and especially men in power are prone to corruption, was to prove a potent force in keeping Americans traveling together in the same direction.

6

The Americans and the Empire

Still another common denominator lay in the fact that most of the inhabitants of every colony made their living from the soil. There were four or five large cities—Charleston, Philadelphia, New York, Newport, Boston—and several more good-sized towns where merchants and tradesmen flourished, but most people north and south lived on land they cultivated. And probably most of them (research has not revealed the exact proportion), especially in the North, owned their land.

This widespread ownership of property is perhaps the most important single fact about the Americans of the Revolutionary period. It meant that they were not divided so widely between rich and poor as the people of the Old World. Standing on his own land with spade in hand and flintlock not far off, the American could look at his richest neighbor and laugh. Though there was as yet no professed belief in social equality, though in every colony there were aristocrats, marked by the fine houses they lived in and the fine clothes they wore, there were no peasants for them to lord it over—except always the slaves. Apart from the slaves the people were much of a piece and did not know what it meant to bow and scrape to a titled nobility.

Ownership of property gave not only economic independence but also political independence to the average American. In every colony that was to join in the Revolution there was a representative assembly, elected by property-holders, which made the laws and levied the taxes. Historians once assumed that the property qualification confined the suffrage to a small segment of the population. But if most men owned property, as now seems probable, then most men could vote.

They enjoyed also a common privilege the meaning of which was more difficult to determine: they were all subjects of Great Britain.

7

The Americans and the Empire

This privilege—and they counted it as such—they shared not only with each other but with people in Canada, Florida, the West Indies, and the East Indies. They were part of the largest empire the Western world had ever known, an empire that in 1763 had just finished defeating its most serious rival, France, in the long and bloody Seven Years' War.

For Americans the great thing about this empire, apart from the sheer pride of belonging to it, was that it let you alone. The average colonist might go through the year, he might even go through a lifetime, without seeing an officer of the empire. His colony had not been founded under imperial direction but by private enterprise operating under what amounted to a license from the King of England. In most colonies the King appointed the governor and gave him directions, but it was one thing to give directions and another to have them carried out.

On paper the governor's powers seemed large, larger even than those that the king enjoyed in the English government. The royal governor of a colony had the right to summon or dismiss his representative assembly at will, and he had a veto power over its every act. But in practice the governor proved a paper tiger. He had virtually no funds to run the government except what he could wheedle from the assembly. He could not do without the yearly taxes it voted, nor could he afford to antagonize the members who did the voting by disallowing legislation they favored. In practice, therefore, he could exercise his seeming powers only cautiously and sparingly; otherwise he might bring his government to a standstill. And though the king could still veto a colonial law that the governor had unwillingly allowed, the assemblies generally managed to get their way in the end. Their control over taxation was a weapon that even their distant monarch was obliged to respect.

The Americans and the Empire

Apart from the royal governors, the only imperial officers normally encountered in the colonies were those charged with enforcing the Navigation Acts. These were acts passed by the British Parliament to regulate colonial trade so that raw materials were produced for the mother country and manufactured goods were purchased from her. The acts required that certain products of the colonies, such as tobacco, rice, indigo, and furs, when exported should be taken only to England or to another English colony; they required that the colonies purchase European manufactures only through England; and they required that all colonial trade be carried in English or colonial shipping. The acts also charged duties to discourage the colonists from importing certain foreign items, granted bounties to encourage them in supplying specific raw products, and prohibited them from some kinds of manufacturing. For example, a bounty was granted on the production of raw iron, but the production of finished iron goods was forbidden (except in those mills already operating when the prohibition was established in 1750).

The purpose of the acts was to promote the economic welfare of the empire in general and of the mother country in particular. The restrictions placed on the colonies to make them serve English interests did not seriously hamper them, because the acts required the same kind of activities that the free play of economic forces would probably have produced anyhow. In America natural resources, especially land, were cheap, while labor (and consequently manufacturing) was dear. In the Old World the situation was reversed. Under these circumstances it was advantageous for the colonists to sell raw materials and buy manufactures. Though they had to buy from England she was the most advanced industrial country in the world and could generally offer the best prices.

The Americans and the Empire

The only Navigation Act that could have caused real hardship was one passed in 1733, placing a duty of sixpence per gallon on molasses imported into the colonies from outside the British Empire. If it had been enforced, the Molasses Act might have crippled the New England rum trade and distilling industry: the duty on foreign molasses was prohibitively high, and the sugar plantations in the British West Indies, for the benefit of which the act was passed, did not produce enough molasses to satisfy the thirst of colonial tipplers or of the other rum drinkers from the fishing banks of Newfoundland to the coasts of Africa. But the act was not enforced. The customs officers who were supposed to collect the duty were a venal lot; and the New Englanders were able to arrange a standard bribe, varying from a half-penny to a penny and a half per gallon, in return for which the officers looked the other way whenever a cargo of French molasses arrived.

Doubtless the collectors were persuaded by similar methods to overlook occasional cargoes of French or Dutch textiles. But if the colonists felt aggrieved by the Navigation Acts, other than the Molasses Act, they did not say so. They did not even complain that the acts were passed by a British Parliament in which they had no representative. It has often been suggested that their contentment was the result of the ineffectiveness of imperial administration, and it must be admitted that the empire was run in a strangely listless manner.

The government of Great Britain had not been designed to cover half the globe, and when Englishmen were not busy extending their possessions still farther, they were apt to regard the problem of turnpikes in Yorkshire as vastly more important than the enforcement of the Navigation Acts in New York. Administration of the colonies was left to the King, who turned it over to his Secretary of State for the Southern Department (whose principal business was

The Americans and the Empire

England's relations with southern Europe). The Secretary left it pretty much to the Board of Trade and Plantations, a sort of Chamber of Commerce with purely advisory powers. The Board of Trade told the Secretary what to do; he told the royal governors; the governors told the colonists; and the colonists did what they pleased.

This system, or lack of system, had at least one virtue: it did no harm, a fact evidenced by the rolling prosperity of mother country and colonies alike. The British Empire, however inefficient its management, was very much a going concern, and wise men on both sides of the Atlantic believed that its success was intimately connected with the bumbling way in which it was run. They saw both the prosperity and the inefficiency of the empire as results of the freedom that prevailed in it. Freedom, inefficiency, and prosperity are not infrequently found together, and it is seldom easy to distinguish between the first two. The British Empire was inefficient, but its inhabitants were prosperous, and they were free.

It was this real and present freedom even more than the long and honorable heritage of it that the colonists cherished. They never tired of praising the government that made it possible, and in doing so they were by no means unique. Englishmen too thought of freedom as the special virtue of their constitution, and the fashionable French philosophers agreed. The peculiarity of English government responsible for this happy result was thought to be the combination of monarchy, aristocracy, and democracy embodied in the King, House of Lords, and House of Commons. During the years since the first American colony was founded, the balance in the combination had altered. The effect of the Civil War of the 1640's and of the Revolution of 1688 had been to reduce the authority of the King and to establish the predominance of Parliament, particularly the House of Commons. In the eighteenth century it had

11

come to be accepted that English liberty depended upon this predominance, and George III, the conscientious farmer who ascended the throne in 1760, never failed to acknowledge the supremacy of his Parliament.

The colonists joined in the applause for Parliament. Though they had not participated directly in its past triumphs, they had enjoyed an analogous experience which they identified, in a way they might not have been able to define, with that of their English cousins. For while Parliament was winning control in England, the colonial assemblies were winning it overseas and had tamed the royal governors almost as effectively as Parliament tamed the King. When Parliament got rid of James II in the Revolution of 1688, New England and New York threw off the new government James had established over them and restored the assemblies he had temporarily suspended. The supremacy of Parliament had thus become associated in the colonial mind with the supremacy of the assemblies. Both stood for English liberty, for laws made by consent of the people. Both meant that Englishmen were freer than all the rest of the world.

The relations of mother country and colony had not been seriously affected by the shifts of power in England. Apart from trade regulations the laws the Americans lived by were made, as always, by their own representatives. Whatever directions came to them from England came, as always, from the King through the royal governors.

What the colonists did not understand was that the King, because of the supremacy of Parliament, did not speak merely for himself when he sent them orders. The orders were in effect Parliament's as much as his. As long as they were sent through the governors, there would be no trouble: the colonial assemblies had learned over the years to deal with governors. But what would

The Americans and the Empire

happen if King and Parliament tired of the independent, not to say truculent, behavior of the assemblies? What if the supremacy of the assemblies were matched, not against the royal governors, but against the corresponding and overruling supremacy of Parliament? Suppose Parliament should decide to carry out its own orders by legislating directly for the colonists as it had admittedly, if rarely, done in the past?

When that happened Americans would have to think again about Parliamentary supremacy and ask themselves whether British freedom really resided there.

13

II

Sugar and Stamps, 1764-66

No one likes to pay taxes, and Englishmen in 1763 thought they had too many. Though they were the most powerful nation in the world and the most prosperous, their government was costing too much. They had just completed the very expensive Seven Years' War against France, doubling the national debt. The war had also left them with a huge new territory to administer: Canada and the eastern Mississippi Valley. Many of them thought the whole of it not worth keeping; and when they heard that the government was going to assign ten thousand troops to defend and pacify it, they could only think of how much that many men would eat and drink in a year and how many uniforms they would wear out and how much they would have to be paid.

The idea of relieving their own burdens by taxing the colonies had often been suggested to Englishmen, but hitherto they had not thought it wise to take the step. Sir Robert Walpole, who was admired and hated as the most astute politician of the preceding generation, was said to have dismissed such a proposal with a smile, saying, "I will leave that for some of my successors, who may have more courage than I have."

George Grenville in 1763 was ready to tread where Walpole had

Sugar and Stamps, 1764–66

feared to. Grenville, a wily and humorless statesman with a head for figures, became Chancellor of the Exchequer in 1763 and discovered from the treasury books that the American customs service was costing more to operate than it was bringing in. He began his pursuit of the American dollar by tightening up the service to prevent smuggling. The Americans in a series of remonstrances at once pointed out that the sixpence duty on foreign molasses was prohibitive and if enforced would ruin an important branch of the colonial economy. They urged that it be discontinued. Grenville had no desire to destroy the New England rum industry but merely to make it furnish a revenue to England. He accordingly decided to continue the duty but cut it in half. Knowing that the colonial merchants were paying up to a penny and a half per gallon in bribes, he reasoned that they could afford to pay threepence in an honest tax.

By early 1764 he had ready a bill which Parliament quickly turned into an act, effecting not only this change but many others, all designed to produce revenue by means of customs duties. Hitherto customs duties had been levied simply for the purpose of directing trade. Now they would also bring in a substantial income to help defray the cost of maintaining troops in America. To put teeth in the act, the whole system of enforcement was overhauled, with an elaborate series of papers to be filled out by shippers for every cargo, and violations to be tried in admiralty courts, which operated without juries (colonial juries were notoriously easy on smugglers). And since he thought the Americans could afford to pay still more, Grenville announced his intention of introducing in the following year a bill for extending to the colonies the kind of stamp duties that Englishmen paid on legal documents, certificates, and other paper items.

The Americans were thus confronted with the first great chal-

Sugar and Stamps, 1764-66

lenge of the Revolutionary period. The new act, usually called the Sugar Act, was in form a revision of the old customs laws; but its purpose was novel, to raise money, and this purpose was frankly stated in the preamble. The colonists had long since learned the importance of the power to tax, from the struggle of their own assemblies with the royal governors and from Parliament's struggle with the King. For them as for other Englishmen, Parliament's exclusive power to tax was the most important feature of its supremacy over the King, the most important guarantee of English liberty. It was for this principle that John Hampden had gone to prison when he refused to pay a tax demanded by the King alone; it was this principle that Parliament had secured when it gave the throne of James Stuart to William of Orange in 1688; and it was this principle that John Locke, the philosopher, had insisted upon in justifying that revolution: men's property must not be taken away without their consent, given either in person or by their representatives. For the colonists, as for other Englishmen, property was not merely a possession to be hoarded and admired; it was rather the source of life and liberty. If a man had property, if he had land, he had his own source of food, he could be independent of all other men, including kings and lords. Where property was concentrated in the hands of a king and aristocracy, only the king and the aristocracy would be free, while the rest of the population would be little better than slaves, victims of the eternal efforts of rulers to exploit subjects. Without property men could be starved into submission. Hence liberty rested on property, and whatever threatened the security of property threatened liberty.

Security for their property was what Englishmen had won in the course of a long history. Parliament was a representative body, and as such it enjoyed the sole authority to grant the property of Englishmen in taxes. But when it presumed on this authority to

16

grant the property of colonial Englishmen, who were not represented in it, then surely something had gone awry, then surely it ceased to be the great protector of popular liberty and became a threat to the freedom of the Americans whose property it demanded.

The Americans were quick to see the threat, but they were not altogether sure what to do about it. Some favored an immediate denial of Parliament's authority to tax them. Others thought it best not to raise this question but simply request with all due humility the repeal of the new duties. In Massachusetts, for example, the assembly drew up a spirited protest in which they stated plainly "that we look upon those Duties as a tax, and which we humbly apprehend ought not to be laid without the Representatives of the People affected by them." The new act, they said, deprived the people of "the most essential Rights of Britons." But before the assembly could send this message, Lieutenant-Governor Hutchinson persuaded them to abandon it in favor of a much milder request for the continuation of the "privileges" formerly enjoyed. The New York Assembly, on the other hand, got off an eloquent series of petitions in which they claimed a complete exemption from Parliamentary taxation, and affirmed their disdain "of claiming that Exemption as *a Privilege*—They found it on a Basis more honourable, solid and stable; they challenge it, and glory in it as their Right."

It was their right not only as Englishmen but as men: "An Exemption from the Burthen of ungranted, involuntary Taxes, must be the grand Principle of every free State.—Without such a Right vested in themselves, exclusive of all others, there can be no Liberty, no Happiness, no Security; it is inseparable from the very idea of Property, for who can call that his own, which may be taken away at the Pleasure of another?" And lest the members of Parliament think that customs duties used for revenue were less objectionable than other taxes, the New Yorkers took care to point out that "all Impositions, whether they be internal Taxes, or Duties paid, for what we consume, equally diminish the Estates upon which they are charged. . . . The whole Wealth of a Country may be as effectually drawn off, by the Exaction of Duties, as by any other Tax upon their Estates."

James Otis, the popular leader of the Massachusetts Assembly, made this same point in a pamphlet published during the summer of 1764. He had evidently heard that some Englishmen thought an "external" tax on trade more permissible than an "internal" or direct tax. He therefore specifically stated, "There is no foundation for the distinction some make in England, between an internal and an external tax on the colonies." And though the Massachusetts Assembly had been willing to tone down its own official protest, it endorsed Otis's pamphlet by formal vote and shipped copies of it off to London.

In London, Grenville was not to be disheartened by these and other colonial objections to his measure. He had one of his subordinates, Thomas Whately, write an answering pamphlet, in which it was acknowledged that English liberty forbade taxation without consent. Whately in fact went even further and denied that any laws whatever could be imposed on British subjects without their consent. But, he insisted, no such thing was involved in the Sugar Act or any other act of Parliament affecting the colonists; for though they were not actually represented in the House of Commons, though they could not vote for any member, neither could most Englishmen. Most Englishmen (at least three-quarters of the adult males) were disqualified from voting by not owning enough property, or by living in towns not entitled to send members, or by archaic local regulations in the towns that did send members. These Englishmen, Whately assured the colonists, were not really unrepresented. They and the colonists, without voting for anyone, enjoyed a *virtual* representation. Every member of Parliament, according to Whately, was there to represent the whole empire and not merely the few electors who happened to choose him.

This specious nonsense was designed to justify not only the Sugar Act but also Grenville's proposed stamp tax, for the colonists in their protests and petitions had objected to both. Grenville went through the motions of suggesting that they tax themselves in lieu of a Parliamentary tax, but the suggestion was never formally communicated and seems to have been only a rhetorical gesture, since he never made known how much he wished each colony to raise. Instead, he commissioned Whately to gather the necessary information and prepare the bill for a stamp tax. This was ready for presentation to Parliament in February, 1765, and in March it became a law.

The Americans had had a year's warning that the act was coming, and the act itself gave them half a year more to think and prepare, for it was not to take effect until November. Though someone in London forgot for several months to send official notice or even a copy of the act to the royal governors and to the officers appointed to collect the duties, the American newspapers carried all the lengthy details early in May of 1765. Almost anything formally written or printed would have to be on special stamped paper which would be shipped from the central stamp office in London and dispensed in America by local agents on payment of specified taxes. The colonists could see that they would have to pay stamp fees at every stage of a lawsuit, that diplomas and deeds, almanacs and advertisements, bills and bonds, customs papers and newspapers, even dice and cards, would all be charged. But there was not much interest in the details: every duty, however large or small, was felt to be an attack on the security of property because it was levied without consent. If Parliament succeeded in collecting the stamp tax, there was no telling how much would be demanded in the future; for America's loss would be England's gain: every penny collected in America would be a penny saved to the constituents of the Parliament that levied the tax.

The colonists therefore did not argue about the details. Instead, they moved against the act itself, to secure repeal if possible, to prevent enforcement whether they got repeal or not. The Sugar Act of the previous year had set in motion an attempt to bring pressure on England by reducing colonial imports of her manufactures. Letters to the editor in various newspapers urged the virtues of homespun and home brew; a society was formed in New York to encourage local manufacturing; and volunteer firemen, who seem generally more interested in politics than in fires, announced in the newspapers that they would increase the American supply of wool by not eating lamb. With passage of the Stamp Act the boycott method of bringing Parliament to terms was taken up seriously by the merchants of the cities. Led by those of New York, they agreed to cease importing all British goods unless the Stamp Act were repealed.

Without waiting for such measures to take effect, the colonists also took steps to see that the Stamp Act should be a dead letter before it began. Grenville had hoped to appease the opposition by selecting native Americans for stamp distributors. Since the men he chose were all men of means, owners of substantial houses, a way of inducing them to reject the office was not hard to discover. Boston showed the way in August, 1765, when a mob stoned and pillaged the house of Andrew Oliver. The following day Oliver was visited by a number of gentlemen who suggested that to avoid further damage and danger he ought to resign the office Grenville had given him, an office which did not promise under the circumstances to be very lucrative anyhow. Poor Oliver knew of his appointment only as his neighbors knew of it, through the newspapers. He had therefore nothing to resign, but he obliged by declaring publicly that he would abandon the office as soon as possible and would do nothing toward executing the act. Some months later when his commission did arrive, the mob made him repeat the performance with a full resignation.

Meanwhile, Bostonians found mobbing so effective a weapon that they used it gratuitously on Lieutenant-Governor Hutchinson, whom they wrongly suspected of advocating the Stamp Act, on the Comptroller of Customs, and on one of the officers of the admiralty court. The other colonies took up the example, and by November 1, 1765, no one in America was prepared to distribute the stamped paper, which was safely stowed away in forts and warships. When that date arrived, there was a pause in business in most colonies as people made up their minds which way to nullify the act: by doing nothing that required the use of stamps or by proceeding without them. Once the latter course was chosen by determined groups of citizens, they found it easy, by the mere threat of mob action, to coerce recalcitrant dissenters including the royally appointed customs officers. Within a few months the ports were open for business as usual with no sign of a stamp (though because of the boycott, cargoes from England were few). The courts too were open, and unstamped newspapers appeared weekly, full of messages encouraging the people to stand firm.

As they went about the work of defying the most powerful government in the world, the Americans had need of encouragement. When word reached England of what they were doing, there was a great deal of talk about putting them in their places. "These yellow shadows of men," cried one frantic London newspaper, "are by no means fit for a Conflict with our Troops: Nor will ever such

Sugar and Stamps, 1764-66

romantic Adventures of Chivalry enter into their trembling Hearts.'' Other Englishmen knew better and said so. Some were sympathetic with the Americans but felt that defiance must be suppressed before mercy could safely be shown.

As for the Americans, they knew that the full weight of the British Army and Navy might soon descend upon them, but they were ready to fight rather than submit. In towns and villages everywhere they formed themselves into associations which they called ''Sons of Liberty'' and declared their intention to resist the Stamp Act, as they usually put it, ''to the last extremity.'' They were ready, in other words, to risk their lives and fortunes in rebellion rather than allow their property to be taken by a Parliament in which they had no representative.

It is of course easier to say you will fight than it is to fight, but the assurance with which the colonists proceeded in their whole nullification of the Stamp Act argues an extraordinary conviction among them that Parliament had no business doing what it was trying to do. Though there had hitherto been little occasion for the expression of such a conviction, it emerged full grown as soon as the Stamp Act was passed. When the Virginia House of Burgesses, sparked by Patrick Henry, adopted a set of resolutions denouncing Parliamentary taxation, other colonial assemblies followed with a speed that showed how wide and how spontaneous was the agreement on this subject. Though Americans could not agree on boundary lines and Indian wars, they could agree without argument on opposition to taxes. At the invitation of Massachusetts nine colonies even sent delegates to a congress in New York in October, 1765, where they formally joined in another set of resolutions and petitions denying the authority of Parliament to tax them.

The resolutions and the actual resistance to the Stamp Act both

22

bespeak a long-standing belief that was merely awaiting utterance; but the utterance was itself an event of the first importance in inaugurating the American search for principles. The problem of putting into words the dimensions of an authority hitherto unmeasured was an experience that set minds roaming along new and unexplored paths. Englishmen frequently spoke of Parliamentary supremacy in absolute terms; the Americans were certain that it had limits short of the right to tax them. But where? Soon after news of the Stamp Act arrived, a widely circulated newspaper article observed: "No Parliament can alter the Nature of Things, or make that good which is really evil.... There is certainly some Bounds to their Power, and 'tis Pity they were not more certainly known." In drafting their resolutions and declarations, the Americans were obliged to survey the bounds and map out, in however crude and tentative a fashion, the area of human freedom.

In making their surveys the leaders of the search found it easy to state the one thing they were certain Parliament could not do: tax people who were not represented in it. The resolutions all state this limitation clearly and without qualification. Now, as in the previous year's protests against the Sugar Act, there was no evidence of the distinction between internal and external taxes which, as we shall see, was later imputed to the colonists. Parliament, they said, had no authority to tax them at all. That authority was reserved exclusively to assemblies of their own elected representatives.

The "virtual" representation that Whately claimed for Parliament was roundly rejected. The Virginia Resolves, for example, spelled out the importance of actual representation by stating "That the Taxation of the People by themselves, or by Persons chosen by themselves to represent them, who can only know what Taxes the People are able to bear, or the easiest Method of raising them, and must themselves be affected by every Tax laid upon the People, is the only Security against a burthensome Taxation, and the Distinguishing Characteristic of British Freedom.'' Pennsylvania declared ''That the only legal Representatives of the Inhabitants of this Province are the Persons they annually elect to serve as Members of Assembly.'' Maryland answered Whately and Grenville directly by stating ''That it cannot, with any Truth or Propriety, be said, That the Freemen of this Province of Maryland, are Represented in the British Parliament.'' Similar denials came from other colonies and from the Stamp Act Congress in New York. Behind them lay a chain of argument that demolished Whately's. Daniel Dulany, a Maryland lawyer, had developed it at length in the best-selling pamphlet of 1765 (*Considerations on the Propriety of Imposing Taxes in the British Colonies*), showing that virtual representation could not be applied to the whole empire but only to Great Britain, where the people who had no right to vote had interests otherwise similar to those of the people who did vote. The interests of Americans, especially in taxation, were apt to be the opposite of Englishmen's and wholly incapable of expression through virtual representation.

Neither Dulany nor the assemblymen who adopted the same reasoning were arguing that Parliament ought to be expanded by the admission of American members. A few Americans, notably James Otis, had suggested this possibility, but others perceived that the suggestion was impracticable. The American representatives would be a small minority, unable to affect the outcome of any issue in which British interests were opposed to American. Their presence would merely justify the kind of oppression the colonists now feared. The Stamp Act Congress therefore expressed the feeling of the great majority when it stated ''That the People of these Colonies are not, and from their local Circumstances cannot be, Represented in the House of Commons in Great-Britain.''

Sugar and Stamps, 1764–66

With the rejection of both virtual and actual representation in Parliament, the road lay open to a radical conclusion, namely, that the colonies were wholly beyond the control of Parliament. A few bold and anonymous souls took hesitant steps along this road. For example, a writer in the *Providence Gazette* of May 11, 1765, who signed himself "A Plain Yeoman" denied any connection between Great Britain and the colonies except "that we are all the common subjects of the same King." Another newspaper article, signed "Phileleutherus," asserted that the members of Parliament had "no more Legislative Authority over us than those that lived before the Flood." But no responsible American statesman was ready as yet to explore such strange territory.

The Stamp Act Congress which convened in New York in October, 1765, acknowledged in its first resolution "all due Subordination" to Parliament, and though the members found it difficult to state exactly what subordination was due, they did raise the question, in their petition to the House of Commons, "whether there be not a material Distinction in Reason and sound Policy, at least, between the necessary Exercise of Parliamentary Jurisdiction in general Acts, for the Amendment of the Common Law, and the Regulation of Trade and Commerce through the whole Empire, and the Exercise of that Jurisdiction, by imposing Taxes on the Colonies." There was a distinction, in other words, between taxation and legislation, and the right to legislate did not necessarily include the right to tax. Taxes were a gift, given by the people through their representatives, and consequently only a representative body could grant them. Legislation, however, might be permissible to a government regardless of its composition. Parliament, because of the representative character of the House of Commons, had powers of taxation as well as legislation for Great Britain, but for the rest of the Empire, which was not represented in the House of Commons, Parliament had legislative powers only.

The colonies found confirmation for this distinction in the fact that the procedure of Parliament in granting taxes was unique: ordinary legislation could originate in either the House of Commons or the House of Lords, but a tax was given and granted to the King by the Commons who alone could initiate it. It was their gift. And for the Commons of Great Britain to give away the property of the King's subjects in America seemed absurd. Thus the Connecticut Assembly declared that "an act for raising money by duties or taxes differs from other acts of legislation, in that it is always considered as a free gift of the people made by their legal and elected representatives; and that we cannot conceive that the people of Great Britain, or their representatives, have right to dispose of our property."

Here then was the boundary of Parliament's authority in America. It could legislate, but it could not tax.

"Legislation" is a big word, and the colonists probably did not intend to attribute unlimited lawmaking power to Parliament. They certainly did not approve legislation curtailing the right of trial by jury, for they condemned as unconstitutional the extension of admiralty jurisdiction over the Navigation Acts. They also stated in the Virginia Resolves and the other resolves modeled on Virginia's that Parliament could not alter the "internal polity" of the colonies, by which they meant the form of government. But the big issue of 1765 was taxation. It would be time enough to place clearer limits on legislation if the need should arise.

This political position was the first stopping point in the American journey. Perhaps it might better be called the starting point, for it was essentially a description of the imperial constitution as Americans thought it had been before George Grenville appeared. Parliament, exercising the powers of legislation, supervised and regulated the trade of the empire but otherwise let the colonists alone and in particular did not tax them. If England had been willing, the colonists would have been happy to settle down again on this position and search no further. They wanted, as yet, no more freedom than they had enjoyed in the past. But they wanted no less, either, and were willing to fight for it.

In 1766 they did not have to fight, because in February of that year England repealed the Stamp Act, and for a time it looked as though the old state of things would be restored.

III

Peace without Honor, 1766-68

When the members of the world's most powerful legislative body repealed the act they had passed less than a year before, it was not because the Sons of Liberty across the water had spread terror among them. Nor was it because colonial assemblymen and pamphleteers had convinced them they were wrong. Insofar as they were moved at all by colonial arguments, they were moved to exasperation, and repeal was engineered only by concealing from them the full extent of the divergence between colonial and British views. How this was done is worth examining, for the misunderstanding begun at this time was never entirely overcome.

There were in Parliament two groups who favored repeal. One was headed by William Pitt, an eccentric and domineering genius who enjoyed a tremendous popularity in both England and America for his successful prosecution of the recent war against France. Pitt was the kind of man everyone turns to in a crisis, and for a time the members of Parliament had allowed him to order them about like a drill sergeant. But once the crisis was over, they tired of his dictation, and though he remained the great popular hero, his influence within Parliament was reduced to a handful of devoted followers. He and his friends favored repeal of the Stamp

Act but would have coated the pill for their fellow-members with gall instead of sugar. Pitt argued in the House of Commons for the distinction between legislation and taxation that the Americans were demanding. He told the members that "taxation is no part of the governing or legislative power." He rejoiced that the Americans had resisted. He demanded not only that Parliament repeal the act but also admit that "it was founded on an erroneous principle."

Pitt's urging that Parliament eat crow made more difficult the task of the other group that was working for repeal. These men, who appropriated to themselves the name of Old Whigs (though virtually all English statesmen, including the King, claimed the name of Whig), were headed by the Marquis of Rockingham. Rockingham was a frail figure of a man, diffident and fumbling as a leader, but he was supported by a larger following than Pitt enjoyed. He was also supported, for the moment, by the King. The King could still exercise some freedom in the selection of his first minister, and in the summer of 1765 he withdrew his support from Grenville and gave it to Rockingham. Rockingham and his friends were known to be opposed to the Stamp Act, but for that matter they were apt to be opposed to anything Grenville sponsored, and the shift in the King's favor had nothing to do with the Stamp Act. Grenville had displeased the King by introducing a regency bill that excluded the King's mother from the government (in case the King should become incapacitated by ill health), and George III was very sensitive about his mother.

Rockingham thus found himself entrusted with the administration of an act he had not approved and that promised to be the devil's own job to enforce. He wished to get out from under it as rapidly as possible, and he was encouraged in this feeling by the British merchants and manufacturers with whom the Old Whigs were closely allied. Though the English economy was in the midst of a long-term expansion, a postwar recession was at this time closing factories, throwing angry and unruly workmen into the streets, alarming merchants and manufacturers alike. Fortunately for the Americans, the recession coincided with their boycott of English goods and produced a frantic demand for repeal.

Rockingham, by taking advantage of this demand, was able to have Parliament deluged with petitions from strictly British sources, appealing for relief from the disastrous consequences of the Stamp Act. The members were much readier to listen to appeals phrased in these terms than they were to the challenging declarations issuing from colonial assemblies. The problem, in fact, was to soft-pedal the truculent American pronouncements and so keep Parliamentary hackles from rising. For this purpose Rockingham found it convenient to table the petitions of the Stamp Act Congress and treat the members to the soothing personal charm of Benjamin Franklin.

Standing before the House of Commons on February 13, 1766, Franklin gracefully answered the questions put to him, including a large number of carefully planted ones, and succeeded in conveying the impression that the Americans were a parcel of devoted children much oppressed by the Stamp Act and much less radical in their demands than they actually were. Seizing upon the distinction between internal and external taxes which some Englishmen evidently thought valid, Franklin asserted that it was this distinction the Americans were making, that they objected only to internal taxes, not to taxes on trade. Most members of Parliament believed him, though they might have known better had they bothered to read the declarations and petitions sent by the colonial assemblies and the Stamp Act Congress. Franklin's testimony was a dangerous piece of deception with unfortunate aftereffects, but it did help to secure the immediate end in view.

Peace without Honor, 1766–68

Even with Franklin's assistance Rockingham could not bring about repeal until he had first arranged for a "Declaratory Act," affirming Parliament's authority. Here too it was necessary to exercise a certain amount of deception. Pitt was the first to suggest such an act. In denying Parliament's right to tax America and demanding repeal of the Stamp Act, he had also proposed that Parliament assert its sovereignty over the colonies in "every point of legislation whatsoever." When Rockingham drafted such an assertion in the form of an act, some of his advisers suggested that it be made to state specifically Parliament's right to tax. But Rockingham preferred to leave this point comfortably vague by merely affirming Parliament's right to make laws and statutes binding the colonists "in all cases whatsoever." By this general phraseology he hoped to pacify the majority of members, who thought the power to legislate included the right to tax anyhow, and yet not offend Pitt and his followers who took the opposite view. As it turned out, the majority were satisfied, but not Pitt. Since he knew that other members of Parliament interpreted the phrase "in all cases whatsoever" to include taxes, he argued for its deletion, and when he could not prevail, he and his friends voted against the declaration which he himself had suggested in almost identical wording.

Repeal of the Stamp Act was thus secured by persuading Parliament that the Americans objected only to internal taxes; and repeal was accompanied by a declaration of Parliament's authority which the members interpreted to include the right to tax but which did not specifically state such a right.

The Americans were overjoyed at repeal, for it seemed to mean the restoration of their old freedom, but they were puzzled by the accompanying Declaratory Act. Was it made on the assumption for which they had been contending, that taxation is not included in the legislative power? In that case it was a full admission of their rights. But if "all cases whatsoever" included taxation, then they were worse off than before. Grenville had rested Parliament's right to tax, and its right to legislate too, on its representative character. The Declaratory Act said nothing about representation but affirmed the naked authority of Parliament without offering any reason. In Boston John Adams wondered "whether they will lay a tax in consequence of that resolution." He did not have to wonder long.

The candles that burned in celebration of repeal had scarcely stopped smoking when the colonists found themselves in a new quarrel with the mother country. The trouble this time arose from another act passed during the Grenville administration, a billeting act that required the colonial assemblies to furnish food and shelter to soldiers stationed within their respective provincial boundaries. This was not a direct Parliamentary tax but an order to the colonial assemblies requiring them, in effect, to tax themselves. Unless they had the right to refuse the order or to comply only in so far as they pleased, the act could be regarded as a form of tax imposed without consent. The assemblies therefore took care to limit their compliance by not extending the full amount of supplies demanded or by offering them as a free gift of their own. The most conspicuous offender was New York, which had the largest number of troops to support.

When word of this new defiance got back to England in the summer of 1766, the Americans lost many of the friends who had stood by them in the Stamp Act crisis. The Rockingham government had gone the way of the Grenville government, and the new ministry was headed by none other than William Pitt, to whom Americans were erecting statues because of his part in repeal. But Pitt was a better friend to America in opposition than he was at the helm. He was feeble in health and feebler still in political "horse *internal external?*

sense." To have given firm direction to his administration, composed of a coalition of factions, would have required a vigor he no longer possessed. During his continued absence at the health resort of Bath, the members went their own ways, and the most energetic of them, the vain and volatile Charles Townshend, dissented openly from the views of his nominal chief.

As Chancellor of the Exchequer, Townshend courted popularity in the House of Commons by hinting that he knew a painless way to get money out of America. Taking him at his word, the House in an irresponsible mood decided to do itself and its constituents a favor by reducing the English land tax, thereby cutting some £ 400,000 annually from the government's revenue. Townshend was thus challenged to tap the golden spring which the members were sure must lie somewhere among their quarrelsome subjects in America. If Townshend could also teach the Americans proper manners, that would be so much the better. Even Pitt himself, now elevated to the peerage as Lord Chatham, was known to be annoyed at the colonial refusal to feed his troops properly.

Townshend revealed his magic formula on May 13, 1767, and on that day the Americans reaped the harvest sown in February, 1766, when Benjamin Franklin persuaded the House of Commons that the colonists objected only to internal taxes. Townshend had already told the House that he thought the distincition between internal and external taxes absurd. He obviously did not know, nor did most of the other members, that the Americans thought it absurd too, for he proposed that out of deference to this supposed American absurdity the colonists be saddled with a full measure of external taxes. Let them pay duties on the items they imported: on glass, lead, paper, paints, tea. And let the duties be collected in America. In order to insure collection let the American customs service be reorganized. Instead of operating by remote control from

Townsh

England, it should be supervised by a separate Board of Customs Commissioners, located at the center of trouble in Boston. And as for the New York Assembly, which still refused to comply fully with the billeting requirements, let the governor be instructed to veto the assembly's every act until it knuckled under. The substance of these proposals was embodied in three bills which Parliament promptly enacted into law.

Americans reacted to Townshend as they had to Grenville. They saw now what Parliament had intended by the Declaratory Act. Since the issue had not been settled by repeal of the Stamp Act, it would be necessary to fight it out all over again, and this they prepared to do. Led by Boston, the people of various towns reaffirmed their fondness for homespun and their detestation of foreign luxuries, particularly tea. The merchants of the various seaports, some enthusiastically and some reluctantly, agreed not to import British goods until the obnoxious duties were repealed. The newspapers were filled with optimistic reports of the progress of American manufactures. And the right of Parliament to tax the colonies was vigorously denied on every hand.

There was no intercolonial congress this time to draft common objections to Parliamentary taxation, but there seemed to be no need for one. The Townshend duties presented the same kind of challenge as the Stamp Act, and the colonial objections had not changed. There was a new popular spokesman for the American view, John Dickinson of Philadelphia. His *Letters from a Farmer* were widely circulated and enjoyed the same popularity that Daniel Dulany's *Considerations* had won during the Stamp Act crisis. But Dickinson added nothing to Dulany's arguments. He merely reiterated with a fresh vigor the propositions that Americans had insisted upon before. He himself as a leading member of the Stamp Act Congress had taken a large hand in formulating those propositions. He was therefore able to give the lie direct to the claim upon which Townshend justified his duties, that the Americans distinguished between internal and external taxes and admitted the constitutionality of the latter. Dickinson quoted the resolves of the Stamp Act Congress and then stated flatly, "Here is no distinction made between internal and external taxes." Dickinson, like Dulany and other writers at the time of the Stamp Act, admitted Parliament's right to use duties, from which an incidental revenue might arise, to regulate trade. What he denied—as they had denied—was the right to levy duties for the purpose of revenue.

So aroused were the Americans by the challenge of Parliamentary taxation that they saw not only the act which levied duties but all the Townshend Acts as measures designed to tax them. They had already identified as a tax the earlier law which required them to provide supplies for imperial troops. The act suspending the New York Assembly for failure to comply confirmed the interpretation. It showed that Parliament was ready to destroy their legislative assemblies in order to carry the point.

The act creating a new Board of Customs Commissioners was obnoxious for the same reason. Americans genuinely, if perhaps unreasonably, felt that there was no need for the additional officers; and as Englishmen worried about the cost of standing armies, Americans worried about the cost of these new customs officers. Their salaries would be paid from the duties they were sent to collect. They would be leeches fattening on the blood of industrious Americans, and if they found enough to feed them, who could tell how they would multiply and how many new taxes would be thought of to satisfy their hunger? It was a plausible line of thought.

The colonists do not seem to have recognized at first that the Townshend Acts presented an even greater threat to their freedom than that of direct or indirect taxation. The full extent of the danger did not become apparent until the customs commissioners set to work at Boston. Professor O. M. Dickerson, the first historian to scrutinize carefully the records of the commission, has called the act establishing it "England's most fateful decision," because most of the events that goaded Americans into independence may be attributed directly or indirectly to it.

It was not that the colonists objected to a more efficient enforcement of the Navigation Acts. In 1768, as we have seen, they were still ready to admit Parliament's right to regulate their trade for the benefit of the mother country; and while they would scarcely welcome anyone who interfered with smuggling, they would not deny that England had a right to interfere. But the new commission was not there simply to enforce the old Navigation Acts. It was there to collect the revenue which Townshend had promised Parliament from America. If the men chosen for this purpose had been saints, they would still have been unpopular in New England. Unfortunately the commissioners who descended on Boston in November, 1767, bore no resemblance to saints. They were a rapacious band of bureaucrats who brought to their task an irrepressible greed and a vindictive malice that could not fail to aggravate the antagonism not only against themselves but also against the Parliament that sent them.

Customs officers in America had always been a bad lot. For thirty years they accepted bribes to overlook illegal cargoes of molasses. After the passage of the Sugar Act it would still have been possible for the officers to look the other way and pocket a modest fee when contraband goods were landed or loaded. But in 1766, as a part of Rockingham's general attempt to pacify the colonies, the duties levied on molasses were reduced from three pence a gallon to a penny. This was no more than the standard bribe, and consequently the collectors could no longer levy a private toll on this item. There lay open to them, however, a new and more lucrative kind of graft, in which they would enjoy the full protection of the law.

Violations of the Sugar Act were punished by seizure of the offending vessel and cargo. Both would be sold and the proceeds divided: a third to the English treasury, a third to the governor of the colony, and a third to the customs officers responsible for the seizure. To an enterprising officer bent on amassing a fortune the prospect of making as many seizures as possible was an inviting one, but before the arrival of the customs commissioners the officers failed to make the most of the opportunity.

To the new commissioners, all of them old hands in the service, belongs the dubious distinction of exploiting the possibilities to their utmost. Professor Dickerson calls their activities "customs racketeering," and they richly deserved the epithet. In the complicated provisions of the Sugar Act it was easy to find technicalities on the basis of which a ship could be seized. The commissioners used these technicalities in a deliberately capricious manner to trap colonial merchants. Their favorite method was to follow a lax procedure for a time and then, suddenly shifting to a strict one, seize all vessels that were following the practice hitherto allowed. By playing fast and loose with the law in this way they could catch the merchants unawares and bring in fabulous sums.

There was very little risk involved for the officers, because the Sugar Act provided that they were to be free from any damage suits if they could show "probable cause" for a mistaken seizure, and the juryless admiralty courts in which cases were tried would generally certify such a probable cause. A merchant, on the other hand, was almost certain to suffer financially no matter how the case came out. Even if he got his vessel back, he would usually have to pay costs of court, and these were frequently so high as to be more than the vessel was worth.

Big merchants and small retailers suffered alike from the rapacity of the officers. Though the Sugar Act was not supposed to apply to movement of vessels within a colony, the small boats that carried firewood and provisions to market were frequently stopped and seized for not having the proper papers. As a result their owners found it necessary to attend at the custom house for every trifling passage, at a cost in fees that hurt them badly and yet added nothing to the King's revenue—the officers were entitled to keep all fees (charges for making out documents) themselves. Even common seamen suffered, for whatever they had in their private chests was now counted as part of the ship's cargo, and they were no longer able to make a little profit on a voyage by bringing back small items for sale.

Americans have never been a patient people, particularly toward governmental officers, and the people of Boston and the other seaports quickly developed an open hatred for the racketeers whom Parliament had sent among them. But the commissioners had ready a remedy for any victims who might fight back. If the colonists should resort to mobbing, they would simply yell for help from the troops so conveniently stationed in America. In fact the commissioners began to yell before they were hit. They had scarcely set up headquarters at Boston when they began writing archly to the English treasury office about their helplessness. The town, they claimed, was in the hands of the mob; without bayonets behind them they would be unable to collect the King's revenue.

In spite of their alleged helplessness the commissioners did not hesitate to undertake what amounted to a vendetta against John Hancock, a well-to-do merchant who showed an open contempt for them from the day of their arrival. They first made a try for him when his ship "Lydia" arrived from London and a zealous minor customs official (a "tidesman") went snooping below decks for smuggled goods. That was a mistake, because tidesmen had no legal right below decks, and Hancock had his sailors pick the man up and dump him unceremoniously on deck. The customs commissioners attempted to file a criminal action against Hancock for this, but the Attorney General of the colony refused to bring the suit, saying that Hancock had acted entirely within his rights.

A month later the commissioners got another chance. On May 9, 1768, Hancock's sloop "Liberty" entered Boston from Madeira, declared a cargo of twenty-five casks of wine, and paid the duty on it. The commissioners were suspicious, because twenty-five casks was below the "Liberty's" capacity, but their own officers found nothing amiss. A month later, however, one of them changed his mind and swore that he had been held captive while large quantities of wine were landed. The story seemed trumped up, because the only other officer on duty could not corroborate it, having been either drunk or asleep at the time. The commissioners nevertheless proceeded to seize the "Liberty."

The result was a genuine riot, in which a mob pelted customs officers with rocks. The commissioners themselves were not present, but they decided to put a safer distance between themselves and the Bostonians. Retiring to Castle William, the fortress in the harbor, they informed the ministry that Boston was in a state of insurrection and that they dared not go ashore. At the same time, not content with seizing the "Liberty," they prepared to bring suit against Hancock and five other merchants for a total of £54,000 in fines for smuggling an alleged £3,000 worth of wine. The charge was so shaky, the only witness so suspicious, that the case was finally dropped, but not before it had given American merchants an idea of what sort of treatment they might expect from the customs commissioners.

The activities of the commissioners looked much different when seen from Westminster than they did at closer range. While the Americans saw their trade and their profits disappearing under the claws of a band of harpies, English statesmen saw an unruly crowd of smugglers fighting against the imposition of law and order. The current political leaders in England were not malicious nor stupid, but they were men of small caliber. Pitt, though still first minister, continued to doze at Bath. Charles Townshend had died at the age of forty-one in September, 1767, and his place as Chancellor of the Exchequer was taken by Lord North, a plodding, stubborn man who was prepared to defend the dignity of Parliament against colonial ruffians at any cost. In January, 1768, the King had created a new office, a Secretariat of State to deal exclusively with colonial affairs, and had given the post to Lord Hillsborough, a pompous, irritable man even more devoted than Lord North to the supremacy of Parliament over the colonies. These two shared with their supporters a belief that the Americans were aiming at total independence from the mother country, that repeal of the Stamp Act had furthered that tendency, and that Parliament must act firmly now or lose the colonies forever. This conviction motivated them in the coming years, and by acting upon it they eventually made it come true.

When the customs commissioners at Boston appealed for troops, Hillsborough was only too ready to believe what they said. Boston, after all, had set off the rioting against the Stamp Act, the repeal of which now appeared to have been a mistake. Boston was where the Massachusetts Assembly met, and Hillsborough was still fuming over a circular letter which the assemblymen had sent in February, 1768, to the other colonies. The letter seemed to Hillsborough an open challenge to the mother country, denying as it did the right of Parliament to tax America. His reaction had been a peremptory order to Massachusetts to rescind it and to the other assemblies to treat it "with the contempt it deserves." But the Boston breed of mischief as usual proved contagious, and the only contempt shown was for him: the other assemblies formally approved the circular letter; the Massachusetts Assembly refused by a vote of ninety-two to seventeen to rescind it. Governor Bernard, on orders from Hillsborough, dissolved the assembly, but the colony continued defiant.

In the face of such conduct the commissioners' screams for help sounded urgent indeed. The members of Parliament were easily convinced that the time had come to teach the Americans a lesson, and for this particular lesson they thought the best qualified instructors would be the regular troops of the British Army. By September, 1768, two regiments were on their way to Boston, with two more soon to follow.

IV

Troops and Tea, 1768-74

For four years now the Americans had been affirming their loyalty to King and Parliament while denying Parliament's right to tax them. They had developed an ingenious and plausible distinction between taxation and legislation, a distinction which described in terms of constitutional right the actual conditions existing before 1763. But in Parliament only William Pitt seems to have adopted their view. Whenever he attempted to explain it to the other members, they simply shook their heads in wonder. "If you understand the difference between representative and legislative capacity it is more than I do," wrote one member to a friend, and his attitude was the prevailing one. An American visiting London heard Lord Hillsborough declare in Parliament that legislation and taxation would stand or fall together, that the notions of the Americans were a polytheism in politics, the most absurd that could be imagined, fatal to the constitution, never to be admitted.

The more the Americans insisted on the distinction, the more determined the members of Parliament became to teach them that they could not set limits on Parliament's authority. It was useless for the royal governor of New Jersey to tell Lord Hillsborough that no force on earth was sufficient to make the Americans admit Parliament's right to tax them. Parliament thought four regiments would be force enough, and indeed the colonists did learn something from the troops, though not quite what Parliament intended.

As the streets of Boston came alive with scarlet coats and the people grew familiar with the rhythm of marching feet, it came to Americans everywhere that a dreadful suspicion had been confirmed. They had thought it strange five years before when they heard that England would maintain 10,000 troops among them to protect them from foreign enemies. Hitherto for more than a hundred and fifty years, while hacking out their farms from a hostile wilderness, they had been left to defend themselves, not only against the Indians, but against the French and Spaniards as well. Only in the recent Seven Years' War had they relied heavily on British troops, and those troops had succeeded in removing their gravest peril, the French menace in Canada. Why at precisely this moment, when the danger had departed, should England decide that they needed a standing army to protect them?

Some Americans thought they knew why, and the reason they suggested was a grim one: England was sending the army not to protect them but to hold them quiet while she extracted their liberties. The suspicion was not wholly unfounded. Although the decision to keep troops in America seems to have been made without much forethought, it had occurred to some of the men involved that the Americans might need watching. Now that the French menace had been removed from their borders, they might feel less dependent on the mother country, might become more self-assertive, might even move toward independence. A few regiments of regulars would dampen the enthusiasm of would-be rebels.

To Englishmen who thought this way the colonial reaction to the Stamp Act was sufficient proof that they were right, that the troops were needed. And to Americans who suspected that the troops were there for sinister reasons the very passage of the Stamp Act was sufficient proof that what they were needed for was to extract American liberties. Everything that followed seemed to confirm suspicions on both sides. Repeal of the Stamp Act momentarily lulled the colonists' fears, but the Townshend Acts renewed them, and the colonists' antagonism to the acts fanned English suspicion of a colonial drive toward independence. Every move by either side seemed to bring the prophecies of the other side closer to fulfillment.

In Boston, even before the soldiers landed, farsighted individuals began to see that the time had come for a reassessment of the colonial position: the distinction between legislation and taxation would not be a sufficient guarantee of liberty against a government that could legislate into existence a horde of racketeers and then support them with bayonets. It might be necessary to look beyond Parliament's right to tax and inquire into the limits of its right to legislate too. On September 13, 1768, with the troops about to arrive, the people of Boston gathered in town meeting and declared their belief that the keeping of a standing army amongst them "without their consent in Person or by Representatives of their own free Election, would be an infringement of their natural, constitutional and Charter Rights; and the employing such Army for the enforcing of Laws made without the consent of the People, in Person, or by their Representatives would be a Grievance." Not content with this challenge to Parliament's legislative authority, some Bostonians wished to back words with weapons if the troops should attempt to land.

To effect a united opposition throughout the colony, Boston called upon the other towns to send delegates to a convention on September 22, 1768. The convention did meet and by so doing

44

demonstrated that the people could not be prevented from expressing themselves through representatives, even though England had dissolved their regular assembly. But the delegates were not yet ready to carry the opposition as far as Boston had done. Disclaiming any official standing, they merely commended their assembly's previous protests against Parliamentary taxation and repeated that "as Englishmen they have an Aversion to an unnecessary Standing Army, which they look upon as dangerous to their Civil Liberty." With this mild declaration the convention adjourned, and on the same day troops came ashore from a fleet of ships which had guns trained on the town. There was no resistance and no disorder.

It would be only a matter of time, however, until the rest of the colony and the other colonies too should see what Boston had begun to see. Throughout America, in coffee houses and taverns, in mansions and farmhouses, the news from Boston was the big news. What was happening there? What was going to happen? The Bostonians, by restraining their anger and offering no open affront to the troops, were able to win universal sympathy and to make the whole policy of employing troops against them seem as ridiculous as it was odious. Ostensibly the soldiers were there to protect the officers of the crown, to quell the mob that was supposed to be endangering law and order. But the mob was conspicuous by its absence. Governor Bernard could read denunciations of himself and the customs commissioners as often as the newspapers appeared. The soldiers could read the hostility of the inhabitants on every face. But no one would oblige with a demonstration of the horrid lawlessness that the troops were supposed to suppress. Bernard could find no pretext for declaring martial law, and even the customs commissioners were unable to stir up a visible danger from which their new guardians might rescue them. In fact, such an embarrassing calm prevailed that no real use could be found for the troops at all—yet no one quite dared take the responsibility for sending them away.

Not until the summer of 1769 did the home government order two of the regiments back to Halifax, and even then two remained behind. As a result it was hard for any American to escape the conclusion that the troops were in Boston not to protect law and order but to overawe the citizens of Massachusetts and prevent them from asserting their natural and constitutional rights while corrupt customs officers plundered their shipping.

The conclusion became all the more reasonable after the soldiers and the customs commissioners allowed themselves to be provoked into the street brawl that became known as the Boston Massacre. Though the Bostonians kept themselves under close discipline, they found many ways of harassing the troops who had come to harass them. Since martial law was not in force, the city magistrates took pleasure in enforcing strictly every law of the province and every bylaw of the town. No doubt the soldiers were prosecuted for every possible breach and probably a good deal more rigorously than ordinary citizens. The people met them with contempt on the streets; children pelted them with snowballs; and the air grew so thick with epithets that it is surprising triggers were not pulled sooner than they were.

On March 5, 1770, there gathered in the square before the custom house a crowd which John Adams later described as "a motley rabble of saucy boys, negroes and mulattoes, Irish teagues and outlandish Jack tars." Before them stood the main guard of the Twenty-ninth Regiment, and behind the soldiers, peering uneasily out the custom-house windows, were some of the men responsible for bringing the troops to Boston. As in all such affrays, it was difficult later for eyewitnesses to agree on how the shooting began. It is clear enough that the soldiers were receiving a heavy bombardment of snowballs and rubbish when they opened fire. Several witnesses thought they heard the command given by Captain Preston. Others saw shots fired from the windows of the custom house. When the shooting stopped, three Bostonians were dead and eight wounded, two of them mortally. No shots were fired at the soldiers.

The story of course lost nothing in the telling as it spread over the Atlantic seaboard. Even the most distant American, reading the embroidered details in his newspapers or hearing them from his neighbor, had to ask himself if his own colony would be next. Those who saw the danger most clearly were publishing plenty of propaganda to make him think so, but Parliament itself had written the best of it. The members seemed obsessed with demonstrating how easily they could dispose of any liberties left in their keeping. When they heard of the unauthorized Massachusetts convention of 1768, they had directed the King to make inquisition at Boston for treason. They were convinced that the resistance to their authority was provoked not by their own inequitable exercise of it but by evil-minded American agitators. A noose around the neck of Samuel Adams and a few others, it was suggested, would be wholesome medicine, and lest a jury of deluded colonists allow the culprits to escape, the trials should be held in England before a special commission. The right to trial by a jury from the vicinage, or neighborhood, of the accused was held sacred by most Englishmen, but Parliamentary leaders easily discovered a legal justification for violating this right. They exhumed a forgotten act passed during the reign of Henry VIII in the sixteenth century. A few of the members were shocked by this proposal to resurrect "an obsolete law which was passed in one of the most cruel and tyrannical reigns." One member said flatly that Americans thus brought to England for trial would rightly be considered as "brought over here to be murdered." But a large majority thought the act well suited to the colonies.

It was aimed, of course, at Boston, for Parliament, following a naïve divide-and-conquer policy, had carefully refrained from investigating opposition to its authority in other colonies. But Americans by now realized that Boston's cause was theirs. They all had property that the British House of Commons was claiming the right to give away. They all had representative assemblies that royal governors might dissolve in favor of Parliament. In Virginia, which had taken the lead in passing resolutions against the Stamp Act, the House of Burgesses drew up a new set, asserting once again their own exclusive authority to levy taxes on their constituents, but going on to expose the violation of right in subjecting Americans to a Parliamentary statute of Henry VIII. Governor Botetourt immediately dissolved the assembly, but the members calmly continued as an extralegal convention and adopted a non-importation agreement to remain in force until all "unconstitutional" revenue acts were repealed. Virginia sent her resolves to the assemblies of other colonies, where again they served as models for more assertions of colonial rights during the summer of 1769.

The Americans still felt most strongly the danger to their liberties from Parliamentary taxation, but they were learning to extend their inquiries to Parliamentary legislation too. They would have been obliged to explore deeper into this territory if England had continued without pause in her efforts to make them bow to absolute authority. But after the proposal to hang a few Bostonians, the ministry and the members of Parliament began to think of tempering authority with wisdom. No one in the ministry thought highly of Townshend's duties: taxes on Britain's exports to the colonies were as disadvantageous to British as to colonial prosperity, and the revenue they brought in was trifling. The Townshend Acts had in fact been passed in a fit of wishful thinking. The only difficulty with repealing them was that by doing so Parliament would seem to be retreating in the face of American resistance.

The solution which occurred to the ministry was to repeal all the duties but one, that on tea. In this way the principle would be upheld, but the substance for the most part given up. Hillsborough notified the colonies that he was going to propose this measure to Parliament and also that the government had no intention of suggesting any more taxes on America for the purpose of revenue. As a further gesture of good will he allowed Governor Bernard to summon the Massachusetts Assembly into meeting again with nothing more said about their refusal to rescind the circular letter. Ten months later, in March, 1770, while Boston was suffering its "massacre," Parliament (now under the leadership of Lord North as first minister) redeemed Hillsborough's pledge by repealing all the Townshend duties except that on tea.

Though memory of the Boston Massacre continued to smolder throughout the coming years, England's concessions resuscitated much of the old good feeling in the colonies and retarded the development of new questions about Parliament's authority. After Parliament enacted its partial repeal of the Townshend duties, the non-importation agreements began to crack. There had been much talk of holding firm until the duty on tea should be removed too, but when New York decided to resume importation (except for tea), the merchants of the other great ports were disposed to follow suit lest they lose all their business to the New Yorkers. The rest of the population, which hitherto had looked to the merchants for leadership, were more ready to continue the boycott; but the whole movement required an extraordinary unanimity in order to be successful, and it quickly broke down.

There followed three years of commercial prosperity in which business was better than ever before and questions of constitutional right were little asked. During this period merchants did import tea and paid the tax on it. They also imported molasses and paid the tax on that. Both these taxes were levied for the purpose of revenue, and it seems appropriate therefore to ask here a question that everyone who examines the American Revolution must sooner or later face: Were the colonists sincere in their declarations of principle or were they merely trying to avoid the unpleasant task of paying taxes that they ought to have paid? This book has proceeded on the conviction that the colonists' attachment to principle was genuine, but it is only fair to say that many historians are inclined to doubt the strength of the attachment. One reason for their doubt is the fact that the colonists submitted to the tea and molasses duties during the period 1770–73.

It is of course impossible to tell why men act as they do. Today we have learned so much of the irrational springs of human behavior from Marx and Darwin and Freud that we are disposed to see all declarations of principle as a camouflage, conscious or unconscious, for some baser motive. But in exercising our new insight we sometimes attribute to the men of previous ages an extraordinary simple-mindedness and demand of them a standard of righteousness which only an angel or a fanatic could meet. If the American colonists were sincere, we say, why did they not state at the outset exactly what they believed and then stick to it without faltering? We forget that to have done so they would have had to know what they believed much better than any of us do and to have adhered to it with a superhuman consistency.

But, it is urged, the principles which the colonists proclaimed were designed simply to further their own economic interests. Can they have been sincere in defending a principle from which they stood to benefit? The colonists would have found this question difficult to understand: the principle of no taxation without representation had been originally invented or discovered by Englishmen who also hoped to benefit from it; and Americans were simply using the principle for its intended purpose. We will see no incongruity in their coupling of principle and self-interest if we will remember that constitutional principles have been created and continue to exist for the protection of the people who live under them. They are seldom referred to unless people fear or feel harm from their violation, and then the greater the harm the greater the clamor. Edmund Burke, who consistently opposed the attempt to tax the colonies, described the origins of constitutional principles when he said that assertions of right were "a sure symptom of an ill-conducted state."

The colonists met the ill-conducted attempt to tax them with an almost unanimous assertion of the principle that taxation was the exclusive right of their own elected representatives. They maintained this principle throughout the Revolutionary period, not simply as an abstract statement of political theory, not simply as a means of evading a particular tax, but as a way of safeguarding the property which they regarded as the only security for life and liberty. Neither the stamp tax nor the Townshend duties were formidable in themselves, but the colonists saw in each the entering wedge of a movement to deprive them of control over their possessions. They fought for that control and obtained repeal of the Stamp Act. With the passage of the Townshend duties they perceived that the British ministry was renewing its attack. As they fought again, they began to wonder whether they were not threatened by Parliamentary legislation as well as taxation.

When the Townshend duties were partially repealed, the threat remained, but it seemed to be much reduced. Lord Hillsborough had declared that there was no intention of taking further revenue from America. His assurance was not the equivalent of a recognition of right, but the Americans had won what appeared to be a partial victory or at least a stalemate. They were still proud to be part of the British Empire. They were prosperous. Reasonable men did not wish to tempt fate by demanding more or to meet conciliation with doctrinaire rigidity. It would take only a little to reawaken their fears of a conspiracy, but surely it is not necessary to impeach their sincerity simply because they showed some degree of flexibility and asserted a principle with less force when the principle seemed to be less in danger.

It would have required a singular tact on both sides to prolong this period of quiescence until mutual suspicions died away. But tact was a rare commodity, among royal officials and colonial politicians alike. A series of incidents beginning early in 1772 led to irreconcilable bitterness and prompted the Americans to a momentous new view of their relation to England.

Despite the peace offerings that England made toward the colonies in 1769 and 1770, there seems to have been no thought of abolishing the American Board of Customs Commissioners. After the Boston Massacre, when the troops withdrew from the city to Castle William in the harbor, the customs commissioners remained behind unabashed and unchastened. The British Navy had placed several warships at their disposal, and in the spring of 1772 one of these, the schooner "Gaspee," was patrolling the shores of Narragansett Bay, exacting a heavy toll from the small vessels which carried wood and provisions along the shores. Farmers and fishermen scarcely dared move a rowboat without taking out bonds. The commander of the schooner seems also to have allowed his men to steal cattle and cut fruit trees for firewood.

As a result of these activities the period of quiescence ceased to be quiet in Rhode Island. The small but far from humble colony had already reached its low boiling point when on June 9, 1772, the "Gaspee," in pursuit of a suspect, ran aground off Pawtuxet a few miles south of Providence. That night a crowd of hard-eyed men from the town, among them its leading merchant, John Brown, swarmed over her sides, took off her crew (wounding the commander who attempted to prevent them), and burned her to the water's edge.

This was not the first revenue ship to be burned in Rhode Island, and the home government decided to investigate what was going on there. A commission was appointed, and six months later, after sitting for seventeen days on the scene, it discovered that no one in Rhode Island knew anything about what had happened. Word had gone round that the commission was empowered to seize suspects and have them transported to England for trial. Though the report was exaggerated, it was all too plausible in the light of Parliament's earlier resurrection of the statute of Henry VIII. The commission actually did nothing; nevertheless, its very existence offended the colonies as much as the burning of the ship offended England.

But even before the "Gaspee" Commission was appointed, England had taken other steps to tighten, as she supposed, the reins of empire. While Rhode Islanders were sullenly viewing the blackened hulk that lay on the sandbar near Pawtuxet, their neighbors in Massachusetts were jolted by a terse announcement from Governor Hutchinson. On June 13, 1772, Hutchinson told the assembly that he neither needed nor would accept any further salary from them, as the King had made provision to pay him from the customs revenues. Shortly afterward it was announced that judges of the Superior Court would likewise receive their pay from the King.

It might be thought that the people of Massachusetts would be glad to escape these burdens, but they understood well that the purpose of the innovations was to free royal officers from dependence on the assembly. The power of the executive would grow accordingly, and the colonists like other Englishmen were conditioned to take alarm at any increase in executive power. While continually affirming their devotion to the best of kings (a distinction accorded to every monarch), they relied on their representative assemblies to stand between them and the orders that the best of kings might issue to them through his governors. If his governors and his judges were to get their salaries from England, then in any future conflict (and the future began to look dark with conflict) between the colonists and the home government, a colonial assembly would be unable to win points by delaying salary appropriations. Governor Hutchinson, who had earned a reputation for rapacity rivaled only by that of his predecessor, Francis Bernard, need no longer fear financial embarrassment in doing precisely what his instructions from England required. The assemblymen told him flatly what they feared would be the result: "a despotic administration of government."

People did not like Thomas Hutchinson. They did not like his long nose or his long face or the long list of offices he held. They did not like his constant courting of royal favor, his unswerving support of England's authority. He was actually an honorable man and a courageous one, but he wore his honor too haughtily and exercised his courage in defying public opinion. Back in 1765, because he was suspected (wrongly) of instigating the Stamp Act, a mob had destroyed most of his house in one of the worst riots in Botson's history. The leaders, who were known, were never punished, and though men of good will shook their heads over the affair, Boston continued to treat him with open hostility. For his own part Hutchinson displayed an understandable concern about the future of royal government—not to mention royal governors—

in Massachusetts and through the years frequently unburdened himself in nervous letters to England, denouncing the villains who were making the path of duty so hard to tread.

During the summer and fall of 1772 Hutchinson rejoiced, and the villains fretted, over his new independence. The principal villain and chief fretter was Samuel Adams, who probably deserved the notoriety he has enjoyed ever since. Adams was as round of face and limb as Hutchinson was gaunt, but the soft lines masked a hard man. Adams went after what he wanted with relentless and frightening singleness of purpose. He was a politician with a politician's sense of timing, and ability to move men where he wanted them to go, and he wanted the people of Massachusetts to go in the direction of independence. He had secretly set his sights on that goal from the moment the troops entered Boston (or so at least he later claimed). He would, of course, have been helpless if the British government had not consistently taken pains to carry out his worst predictions; and during the period of quiescence he did lose much of his influence. But the new arrangement about the governor's and judges' salaries so alarmed people that by November, 1772, they were ready to follow him in a measure that proved to be the most effective means yet discovered by the colonists for mobilizing public opinion.

This was the creation by the Boston town meeting on November 2, 1772, of a Committee of Correspondence. The business of the committee was to prepare a statement of colonial rights, list violations (past, present, and future), communicate these to other towns, and invite similar statements from similar committees in return. Boston was proposing, in effect, a revival of the local Sons of Liberty who had organized in 1765 to proclaim their rights and to nullify the Stamp Act. But where the Sons of Liberty had been extralegal, the committees of correspondence would have the official blessing of the town meetings. The Boston Committee produced its first report (which Adams wrote) on November 20, 1772. It was a ringing denunciation of a dozen ways in which England had violated colonial liberties. ''The colonists,'' it said, ''have been branded with the odious names of traitors and rebels, only for complaining of their grievances; how long such treatment will, or ought to be borne, is submitted.'' Boston adopted the words and sent them on to the other towns. The response was instantaneous, and the press was shortly filled with similar declarations from every side, each one seemingly more bold than the last.

While the towns were thus spurring each other to indignation, a ship was bearing toward them from London with a packet of letters that would make them all gasp. The letters were not new. They had been written in Massachusetts several years before by various highly placed officials, and among them were several in which Thomas Hutchinson bewailed the seditious disposition of that colony. Benjamin Franklin, serving as London agent of the Massachusetts Assembly, had somehow got hold of them and in December, 1772, shipped them back to his constituents.

Though Franklin specified that they must not be published, they were quickly spread over the newspapers, where everyone who could read (and the Massachusetts villains had a notably high rate of literacy) might see that the colony's treatment by the home government was no more than its governor had asked for. The outcome was a new burst of hatred for Hutchinson but even more for the home government that had made his letters the basis of policy while colonial petitions lay unread and unanswered.

It was in the midst of these developments that the Gaspee Commission began its sessions in Rhode Island, and America vibrated again with the sense of danger that had been so acute in 1765. The committees of correspondence spread from Massachusetts to other colonies, and in March, 1773, a proposal went out from the Virginia House of Burgesses to concert the movement on an intercolonial basis. As a result, by the summer of 1773 the colonists were waiting tensely for Parliament's next move, ready to tell each other at once if they thought it dangerous.

The next move, which completely ended whatever quiescence remained, was made with the intention not of disciplining the colonies but of relieving the troubles of the East India Company. This mammoth corporation, which represented England's investment in India, was in financial difficulties. During the preceding three years the government had made various attempts to get it on its feet, but the ailing giant continued to decline. Lord North now decided to help it sell a large quantity of tea in America. The colonists were known as confirmed tea drinkers. In spite of the Townshend duties they were importing substantial quantities of the stuff through legal channels. It was estimated, however, that they smuggled in much more from Holland. Smuggled tea was cheaper because legal tea paid duties both in England and in America and also had to pass through several hands, each of which exacted a profit. The East India Company had been forbidden to sell directly to retail merchants. Instead, it sold at auction to English wholesale merchants who then sold to American wholesale merchants who in turn sold to retail merchants. By the Tea Act, which Parliament passed in May, 1773, the company was permitted to appoint its own agents in America who could distribute tea directly to retailers, thus eliminating whatever profit had been taken by English and American wholesale merchants. At the same time, all English duties on tea exported to America were eliminated, leaving the Townshend duty, collected in America, as the only tax.

The reduction in price which these privileges made possible would enable the East India Company to compete with smuggled tea and obtain a firm control (in which American merchants would have no share) of the American market. The merchants, it will be remembered, had withdrawn from the forefront of resistance to Parliament after the partial repeal of the Townshend duties in 1770. Now they rushed forward again crying "Monopoly" and with that frightening word persuaded the rest of the population that the company's low-priced tea would be only a token of bondage. The American people, they said, were being bribed into paying the tea duty. Once the local merchants were run out of business by the East India Company, the price would be jacked higher than ever, and the tax with it.

The committees of correspondence spread the alarm, and consequently the ships which brought the first consignments of tea late in 1773 were greeted everywhere by determined bands of citizens who urged the captains to turn about and go back whence they came. In most cases the captains agreed, but in Boston Governor Hutchinson, still smarting over the publication of his letters, decided to stage a showdown: he would not permit the ships to leave the harbor without unloading their cargo. The people of Boston and the surrounding towns took up the challenge and on the night of December 16, 1773, unloaded the tea themselves—into the harbor.

With the Boston Tea Party the patience of the ministry abruptly ceased, and in March and April, 1774, an angry Parliament enacted a series of laws, known as the Coercive Acts, to bring the bumptious Bostonians to their knees. The first act closed the port to all commerce. The second altered the Massachusetts government by giving the King, instead of the assembly, the power of appointing the Governor's Council. It also forbade town meetings except for the election of town officials. The third provided that any magistrate, customs officer, or soldier indicted for a capital offense within the colony could be brought to England or Nova Scotia for trial, where he would not have to face a hostile local jury. The fourth provided for the quartering of troops once again within the town of Boston. To carry these acts into effect General Gage, commander-in-chief of British forces in North America, was commissioned as governor of Massachusetts.

Though again the blow was aimed at Massachusetts and especially at Boston, the other colonies were expected to learn from it that Boston had been wicked and was receiving a merited thrashing. Instead, they concluded that Boston was martyred because it stood foremost in defense of colonial rights, and they took up collections and showered the beleaguered city with provisions. Their suspicions of England's motives increased when Parliament, with an unfailing instinct for bad timing, chose this moment (June 22, 1774) to pass an act establishing in the conquered Canadian province of Quebec (under military rule since 1763) a civil government with no representative assembly and with special privileges for the Catholic church. This was bad enough in itself, but the Quebec Act, as the measure was called, extended the boundaries of the province into the Mississippi Valley as far south as the Ohio River. New York, Pennsylvania, and Virginia henceforth would have at their borders a government conducted entirely without the consent of its subjects, a close and constant reminder of what all the colonists now felt sure was in store for them should they fail to surrender their property whenever Parliament demanded it.

While Americans pondered the significance of this, the Bostonians, not at all repentant for their sins, adopted a solemn league and covenant against all trade with Great Britain and invited the other colonies to join in it. Thanks to the committees of correspondence, the proposal received prompt consideration, but before taking action some colonies thought it advisable to get together in an intercolonial congress. This suggestion prevailed, and in September, 1774, the first Continental Congress met at Philadelphia.

V

Equal Rights and Equal Men,
1774-76

Fifty-five men rode into Philadelphia in September, 1774, and began at once to take each other's measure, at dinner parties and breakfasts as well as on the floors of Carpenter's Hall. John Adams sized them all up: John Rutledge of South Carolina ("his appearance is not very promising"); William Livingston of New Jersey ("nothing elegant or genteel about him . . . but very sensible and learned"); and Charles Thomson ("the Sam Adams of Philadelphia"), who was elected Secretary of the Congress at its first meeting even though he was not a delegate.

While John Adams was ticking off the members in this fashion, ·his cousin, the real Sam Adams, was already at work pulling the wires he had learned to manage so dexterously in Boston. Those delegates who had hoped the Congress would take a humble tone were dismayed to see how quickly his influence made itself felt. "He eats little," observed Joseph Galloway of Pennsylvania, "drinks little, sleeps little, thinks much, and is most decisive and indefatigable in the pursuit of his objects." Skilfully prodded by Adams, the Congress began its work by approving the "Suffolk Resolves"—so called because they had been adopted September 6 by a convention in Suffolk County, Massachusetts—which daringly declared that no obediance was due to the Coercive Acts.

With the members already committed to so radical a position it was a foregone conclusion that they would adopt the non-importation, non-exportation, non-consumption agreement they had met to consider. They did so on October 20, but first they engaged in a more significant activity, a reassessment of their relation to the mother country. In the debates on this subject they discovered how far they had travelled in the nine years since the Stamp Act Congress. The delegates to that meeting had agreed that Parliament had no right to tax Americans, but only the rashest proposed to set limits on its legislative authority. Now the question was whether Parliament had any authority in the colonies at all. Many Americans had arrived long since at the conclusion that it did not.

They had reached this point with the aid of Parliament itself. Englishmen had derided and denounced their distinction between legislation and taxation, and Parliament convincingly demonstrated that their liberty could be destroyed as easily by the one as by the other. What no one showed them (and few attempted) was why Parliament should have a right to either. Grenville had once claimed that Americans were subject to Parliament because they were "virtually" represented in it, but this argument was reduced to rubble by Daniel Dulany. Nothing had since been offered to take its place except the Declaratory act, in which the members of Parliament assured themselves that they had the authority by announcing that they had it. If anyone thereafter wanted to know where it came from it came from the announcement!

Faced with this impenetrable assumption of omnipotence, the colonists gradually reacted with an equally absolute but somewhat more rational denial. Parliament, they believed from the beginning, had no authority to tax them, because they were unrepresented. By the same token, if legislation and taxation were indivisible, Parliament had no right to legislate, and so no authority at all over them.

How the claim of absolute authority generated its opposite may be seen at closer range in Massachusetts. When the committees of correspondence in the various towns there began to list their grievances, Governor Hutchinson was alarmed to see how extensively they denied the validity of Parliamentary legislation. He decided to recall them to their senses by another affirmation of their total subordination, with more arguments than Parliament itself had hitherto deigned to offer.

In January, 1773, he read the House of Representatives a long lecture on the subject. "I know of no line that can be drawn," he told them, "between the supreme authority of Parliament and the total independence of the colonies." Hutchinson was the learned author of a history of the colony; and well aware of the American reverence for historical precedent, he drew upon his authority as a scholar to demonstrate that the founders of the colony had always acknowledged the supremacy of Parliament. But Hutchinson was up against a sharper wit and a keener mind than his own.

The House in drafting its answer called upon John Adams, a lawyer from Braintree, more learned in the law than his cousin Samuel and quite as learned in history as the governor. With his assistance an argument was prepared which showed that the founders of the colony had supposed themselves beyond the control of Parliament—and showed it by citations from Hutchinson's own history. With devilish ingenuity Adams even pointed out how the very King who granted the colony's first charter had supposed the same thing. The King, of course, was Charles I, who tried to do away with Parliament altogether! From here the answer went on with relentless logic to turn the governor's own words against him:

"Your Excellency tells us," it said, "you know of no line that can be drawn between the supreme authority of Parliament and the total independence of the colonies. If there be no such line, the consequence is, either that the colonies are the vassals of the Parliament, or that they are totally independent. As it cannot be supposed to have been the intention of the parties in the compact, that we should be reduced to a state of vassalage, the conclusion is, that it was their sense, that we were thus independent." Independent, of course, meant independent of Parliament, not of the King.

Hutchinson had maintained that if the colonies threw off Parliamentary supremacy, they would form distinct kingdoms like England and Scotland. "Very true, may it please your Excellency," replied the committee, "and if they interfere not with each other, what hinders, but that being united in one head and common Sovereign [the King], they may live happily in that connection, and mutually support and protect each other?" When the House of Representatives adopted this reply to the governor as their own, they committed the whole province to the very position that Hutchinson had hoped to forestall, that Parliament had no authority in the colonies whatever.

Hutchinson and the Adamses, in their different ways, brought Massachusetts to this point in 1773. Other Americans reached it in other ways and at other times. Benjamin Franklin got there as early as 1766 and waited quietly for his countrymen to catch up. Another Pennsylvanian, James Wilson, found his way to it in 1770 but refrained from saying so until he heard of the Coercive Acts. Then in a persuasive pamphlet he pointed out the short and easy route to others: the arguments against Parliamentary taxation would apply with equal force to all its legislation.

At Philadelphia in 1774 many of the delegates had followed one route or another to a total repudiation of Parliament, but for some the question of trade regulation remained an obstacle. They felt that for the benefit of the whole empire and of England in particular, as mother country and protector of the seas, there ought to be some central direction of imperial trade and that Parliament was entitled to the job. Others, like Galloway, thought a total reorganization of the empire was necessary, with an American Parliament, subsidiary to the English Parliament, empowered to oversee all intercolonial matters. The Congress, after considering Galloway's plan for a day, voted to table it (and on the last day of the meetings rejected it). Instead they defined their relationship to Parliament in an ambiguously worded resolution worked out by James Duane of New York and by John Adams.

> That the foundation of English liberty, and of all free government, is a right in the people to participate in their legislative council: and as the English colonies are not represented, and from their local and other circumstances, cannot properly be represented in the British Parliament, they are entitled to a free and exclusive power of legislation in their several provincial legislatures, where their right of representation can alone be preserved, in all cases of taxation and internal polity, subject only to the negative of their sovereign, in such manner as has been heretofore used and accustomed. But, from the necessity of the case, and a regard to the mutual interest of both countries, we cheerfully consent to the operation of such Acts of the British Parliament, as are bona fide restrained to the regulation of our external commerce, for the purpose of securing the commercial advantages of the whole empire to the mother country, and the commercial benefits of its respective members; excluding every idea of taxation, internal or external, for raising a revenue on the subjects in American without their consent.

In this equivocal declaration the members with one breath denied the right of Parliament to legislate for them and with the next volunteered to abide by that wonderful old state of things that existed in 1763. In such a mood of reluctant defiance they broke up on October 26, 1774, after providing for another congress in the following spring.

As they prepared to cast off the authority of Parlaiment, Americans were genuinely eager to keep their grip on the past. They had ransacked English and colonial history for precedents to justify their constitutional position, to show that they were still true to the traditions of Englishmen; and they had been remarkably successful in finding the precedents they wanted. But while they clung so persistently to the past, they were actually moving, if only half consciously and unwillingly, away from it. They were in fact on the verge of a discovery that would turn the course of history in a new direction, a discovery that is still reverberating among us and liberating us from our past as it was soon to liberate them, in spite of themselves, from theirs.

This discovery was nothing more or less than the principle of human equality. In 1774 the Americans may not have realized how close they were to it, but there were others who perceived, however dimly, that the whole course of their resistance to Parliament was leading them in that direction. As early as 1767 the French chargé d'affaires in London, following closely the British family quarrel, remarked that the Americans did not aspire to independence but simply to equality of rights with the mother country. The Frenchman's analysis was correct, but he did not dream how far beyond this the demand for equality might carry a people. Lord North was more perceptive. "I can never acquiesce," he said in 1770, "in the absurd opinion that all men are equal." He was talking at the time about the pretensions of the London rabble in petitioning Parliament, but he rightly sensed what that absurd opinion could do to the authority of Parliament, whether in England or America.

The colonists had not voiced such an opinion, even to themselves, when Lord North spoke, and with tactful treatment they might still have been prevented from reaching it. By 1774 they were perilously near it. As long as they stopped their objections to Parliament's authority short of a wholesale rejection, they were accepting a smaller degree of freedom than their brethren in England; but when they repudiated Parliament altogether, they elevated their own assemblies to equal rank with it and themselves to an equality with all the King's subjects in Great Britain. From this position it would be only a short step to the abusrd opinion that Lord North so rightly feared.

Lord North, if he had known how, would have liked nothing better than to return to 1763, as the colonists themselves were urging. And his new Secretary of State for the Colonies, the Earl of Dartmouth (who replaced Hillsborough in 1772), felt the same way. But the road back, as these statesmen saw it, was barred by colonial denials of Parliamentary authority, denials not merely in words but in flagrant resistance. What was worse, the colonists were busy building more road blocks. The very meeting of the Continental Congress appeared as a challenge to Parliament, and congressional measures, however hesitant, as outright treason. Inside Parliament only Pitt and his small following would question the authority to tax, and even Pitt was strong for Parliament's legislative authority. The only conciliatory gesture that North could prevail upon himself and the other members to make was a proposal, passed in February, 1775, that the colonists tax themselves in lieu of a Parliamentary tax. This was merely a repetition of the gesture that Grenville had made in advance of the stamp tax, and it was still as vague and undefined, still as unacceptable, as it had been then.

After pausing for this futile aside, Parliament pressed ahead with its catastrophic instruction of the colonists in the meaning of its authority. With enthusiastic majorities it passed a bill to restrain the entire trade of New England and exclude her from the Newfoundland fisheries. And as the members debated further educational devices, the New Englanders bought gunpowder. On April 19, 1775, they used a good deal of it on the road from Concord to Boston.

The men who faced the British at Lexington Green that morning were part of the Massachusetts militia. Every colony trained its able-bodied men in a militia system for defense against Indians or foreign invasion. When no danger was in the offing, training day was a boisterous holiday, accompanied by light talk, heavy drinking, and precious little training. After Parliament passed the Coercive Acts, the festivities gave way to serious marching and maneuvers. In Massachusetts special companies of "minute-men" were formed to assemble at a moment's notice against the danger that threatened not from the Indians but from the troops that were guarding what was left of England's authority in Boston. The danger materialized on April 19, 1775, when the British marched to Concord, intent on seizing powder and guns stored there by the Americans. Shooting began, almost by accident, at Lexington, but the shots that started the British on their way back from Concord were nobody's mistake. Minute-men and militia closed in on the line of march from all sides and peppered the British columns as they reeled toward Boston. After the last redcoat entered the city, the militia encamped outside it, and the siege of Boston began.

When the Second Continental Congress assembled on May 10, 1775, the members found themselves conducting a war and voted to raise a regular army, of which it was hoped the forces encircling Boston would form the nucleus. To command this "Continental Army" Congress chose not a New Englander but a Virginian, George Washington, and he hurried off to Massachusetts to take charge. Even before he arrived, the militiamen gave the soldiers in Boston one of the worst days in the history of the British Army. On the night of June 16 the Americans invested Breed's Hill, adjacent to Bunker Hill in Charlestown, overlooking Boston. When the British decided to remove them the next day, the result was an unbelievable slaughter of the redcoats who came marching up the hill in close order. In the Battle of Bunker Hill, as it was called, the British showed a courage that wiped out the stain of their hurried retreat from Concord two months before; they kept coming until the Americans ran out of ammunition, and when the day was over the English regiments held the hill. But it would be a long time before they attempted another frontal assault on the raw militia whom they had thought to topple so easily.

Gunpowder is a great equalizer, and after the Americans had matched their muskets against the British, they were more confident than before in denying the authority of Parliament. But there still existed among the members of Congress a forlorn hope that the situation might somehow be retrieved. Though they had had enough of Parliament, and would fight rather than submit to its laws, some of them thought that it might be possible to maintain loyalty and subordination to the King. If their assemblies could be recognized as co-ordinate with Parliament, Americans might still join with Englishmen in subjection to a common sovereign. In this hope, while they prepared to seek foreign aid and organized for an extended war, the members addressed a last petition to George III— the Olive Branch Petition, it was called—urging him to prevent the efforts of Parliament under a corrupt ministry to enslave them.

The Americans did not yet realize that the King was an Englishman of only moderate abilities and a vision that reached no farther than that of his ministers and his Parliament. In the preceding ten or twelve years the members of Parliament had demonstrated that they were unfit to rule an empire. They were, in fact, what the most recent historical scholarship has shown them to be: parochial and provincial. Though in theory each member was supposed to represent the whole kingdom (Grenville had said the whole empire), actually they were wedded to local interests in their particular boroughs and counties. They did not even have a sufficiently large vision to associate in political parties on a national scale. The whole business of parliament seldom rose above the level of logrolling.

The man who kept the logs rolling was the King. In the absence of any better politician it was he who brought miscellaneous factions together to form a working majority for whatever measures he and they could agree on. George III was good at the job, but he was no bigger than the men he managed. In order to play the role the colonists assigned him, he would have been obliged to abandon the one he was engaged in and stand entirely above Parliament. It might even have been necessary for him to resume the veto power and disallow bills in which Parliament sought to legislate for the colonies.

Had he wished to do this, he could scarcely have succeeded, and the few friends of the Americans in Parliament would have been the first to denounce the attempt as a resumption of Stuart tyranny. George III, however, had no such wish. Though he wanted desperately to keep his American colonies, he was wholeheartedly committed to the supremacy of Parliament and ready to go any length to defend it against his rebellious subjects. While the Continental Congress prepared its last appeal to him, his ministers negotiated for 20,000 Russian mercenaries to accomplish what the regular troops in Boston seemed unable to do. When the Czarina refused to hire out her subjects, the ministers satisfied themselves with Hessians instead. The King himself treated the Olive Branch

Petition with contempt. Two days after its arrival in August, 1775, he issued a proclamation declaring the colonies in rebellion, and in December he agreed to an act of Parliament prohibiting all intercourse with them and commanding the seizure of their ships on the high seas. Americans would evidently have to choose between their rights and their King, and in spite of everything the King had done or failed to do, the choice was not easy. While they were gathering their courage to make it, a new voice spoke out in words that imparted all the courage needed—the voice of Thomas Paine, an Englishman who had appeared in Philadelphia less than a year before Bunker Hill. In January, 1776, he published a piece called *Common Sense* which was immediately read throughout the colonies. It was read because it said superbly all the things that Americans were waiting to be told.

The colonists were only fooling themselves, Paine said, if they hoped to enjoy freedom under George III. Not only was the King as bad as his ministers and his Parliament; he was worse; he was the author of their troubles.

The ruler Paine described may not have been the real George III. It may be, as modern scholars have emphasized, that George was playing the only role a responsible monarch could play in the existing situation of politics in Great Britain. But if British politics demanded such a monarch, it was high time for the colonies to cut loose. If Paine misconstrued the motives of the King, he did not misconstrue the facts: there was simply no room in the existing British Empire for a people who wanted the rights that Americans demanded.

Paine, however, did not deliver his message in sadness; his mission was not simply to destroy a lingering faith in the House of Hanover but to liberate Americans from the very idea of monarchy. Hitherto the demand for equality had found expression in assertions that equated Americans with Englishmen. Englishmen were taxed only by consent; therefore Americans must be. Englishmen had a right to be represented in their own legislative body; therefore Americans should have such a right and their assemblies be co-ordinate with Parliament. But Paine made bold to extend the inquiry. Why, he asked, should any man be exalted above others as a king was? "Male and female," he said, "are the distinctions of nature, good and bad the distinctions of Heaven; but how a race of men [hereditary kings] came into the world so exalted above the rest, and distinguished like some new species, is worth inquiring into, and whether they are the means of happiness or of misery to mankind." The result of his inquiry was to show that the only basis for hereditary monarchy is usurpation. "The plain truth," he announced, "is that the antiquity of English monarchy will not bear looking into," or for that matter any monarchy. Nothing but misery had come from kings.

Paine's boldness was breathtaking, and many colonists drew back in horror from the abyss of anarchy toward which his conclusions seemed to lead them. There were in 1776, as there always are, conservative men who thought the overthrow of a government, however evil, must entail worse consequences than submission. They had come this far in seeking what they considered their legal and constitutional rights, but to go where Paine was leading was to abandon both law and constitution and risk all in the untried and unrigged ship of "natural" rights. Rather than board such a vessel they would give up the contest and accept whatever King and Parliament chose to give them.

Many Americans, however, had learned from history that governments deserve no such reverence. In the 1640's Englishmen deposed their king, and in 1688 they did it again. After the first deposition a political philosopher, James Harrington, explained what had happened in his *Oceana*, a book that Americans still studied. In Oceana (England) most of the property, originally in the hands of the king and his nobility, had gradually passed into the hands of a much larger segment of the population. And whoever owns the property, Harrington taught, will sooner or later own the government. In 1649, as Harrington saw it, the people who owned the property of England deposed the king and began to take charge of the government.

Their action proved premature. Monarchy and aristocracy turned out to be stronger than Harrington had supposed, but he gave the people (or at least those who owned property) the nerve to think that they might own their own government. And they vindicated his judgment in 1688 when they again got rid of a king and replaced him with one who would understand that he governed only with their consent. By this time Harrington was dead (after years of imprisonment), but another philosopher, John Locke, in a book that became even more popular than Harrington's, explained to his countrymen why they had every right to fashion their own government.

Locke

Men, Locke said, are by nature free, equal, and independent of each other. In a "state of nature" each man began with the possession only of his own body. But by applying the labor of his body to the land, each transformed what was formerly common into his own private property. In order to protect themselves and their hard-won possessions from attack by wicked individuals, men would agree in a social compact to end the complete independence that existed in the state of nature and to form a society under the supervision of government. Government therefore is instituted by consent of the governed for a definite purpose, and if any particular government fails to fulfil that purpose, it should be replaced by one that will.

73

Equal Rights and Equal Men, 1774-76

Harrington and Locke were popular reading in America, perhaps more so than in England, because what they said made more sense in America. When Locke described his state of nature, he could explain it most vividly by saying that "in the beginning all the World was America." And indeed many Americans had had the actual experience of applying labor to wild land and turning it into their own. Some had even participated in social compacts, setting up new governments in wilderness areas where none had previously existed. And if Harrington was right in thinking that the wide distribution of property in England was what gave the people of England control of their government, Americans knew that their property was much more widely distributed; and in their representative assemblies they let it be known that they expected government to stick to its proper business of protecting them and their property.

During the years of controversy from 1763 to 1776 the colonists studied Locke and Harrington closely (along with subsequent writers like Thomas Gordon, John Trenchard, and James Burgh, who carried on the tradition of Locke and Harrington). And as they tried to define the constitutional limits of British authority, they had ever in mind the elemental principles by which the political philosophers taught them to measure a government's performance. They regarded the rights they demanded not simply as constitutional rights but as natural rights which it was the very purpose of government to protect. They made their demands both as men and as Englishmen, for the English government had been the pattern for Locke's study; and hitherto, at least, Englishmen and English colonists almost alone among the peoples of the world actually did enjoy the rights which Locke believed all men were entitled to.

When the Americans prepared to resist rather than submit to a government that had exceeded its authority, elemental principles became increasingly relevant. As early as the Stamp Act crisis, colonial writers began disussing the process of dissolving government, and the Sons of Liberty prepared to put the ideas into practice. The group at New London, Connecticut, for example, resolved on December 10, 1765: "1st. That every Form of Government rightfully founded, originates from the Consent of the People. 2d. That the Boundaries set by the People in all Constitutions, are the only Limits within which any Officer can lawfully exercise Authority. 3d. That whenever those Bounds are exceeded, the People have a Right to reassume the exercise of that Authority which by Nature they had, before they delegated it to Individuals."

Ten years later, after fighting began, while they continued to hope against hope that England would recognize and restore their constitutional rights, Americans were talking more and more about the state of nature, the origin of government, the limits of authority, and the rights of man. All these ideas were fused in Thomas Paine's denunciation of monarchy. At one stroke he propelled Americans into the great discovery of human equality toward which they had been moving unwittingly ever since they first denied Parliament's right to tax.

There is an exaltation, an excitement, about *Common Sense* that conveys the very uncommon sense of adventure Americans felt as they moved toward independence. With it would come new perils, but also new opportunities, new freedoms. They knew they were on the threshold of a great experience not only for themselves but perhaps for the whole world. "The cause of America," Paine told them, "is in a great measure the cause of all mankind." And they believed him.

On May 15, 1776, the Virginia House of Burgesses voted to instruct its delegates in Congress to propose independence, and on the same day the Congress adopted a resolution sponsored by John

Adams, advising the various colonies to assume complete powers of government within themselves. On June 7 Richard Henry Lee, following the instructions of his Virginia constituents, moved a resolution formally declaring the colonies independent. On July 2 this resolution was adopted and two days later the famous declaration to the world, drafted by Thomas Jefferson.

The Declaration did not go as far as Paine had gone: it was directed only against the "present" King of Great Britain and would not have precluded a monarchical form of government for the United States or for any of its constituent parts. But the Declaration, like *Common Sense*, was much more than a repudiation of George III. It put into words, even more effectively than Paine did, the principle which had been forming in the American mind, "that all men are created equal." The only immediate application was the assertion that Americans were entitled to "a separate and equal station" among the nations of the earth, but the words were phrased in the form of a sacred creed and with an elemental eloquence that has been moving men ever since. The declaration that all men were created equal might mean for the moment that Americans should have the same independence as a nation that other peoples enjoyed. What else it might mean remained to be seen. During the exciting years that lay ahead, as they took their new and independent way, Americans would begin to find out.

Meanwhile they had a job to do.

VI

War and Peace, 1776-83

The men who fixed their signatures to the Declaration of Independence would not have done so without some expectation of success. They knew that they and their countrymen would have to defeat the world's most formidable military and naval power, but in July, 1776, this did not look like an impossible task. They had had plenty of evidence in the preceding decade of the corruption and incompetence of British political leaders, and the events of the preceding year seemed to demonstrate that these men would be no better at running a war than they were at running an empire. On April 19, 1775, the uncoordinated militia of the towns of eastern Massachusetts had routed a considerable body of British regulars. Two months later, at Bunker Hill, the same militia met a frontal assault by British troops and punished them terribly. In March, 1776, after Washington took command and obtained some heavy guns, he was able to force British troops to evacuate Boston and withdraw to Halifax, Nova Scotia.

Against these facts had to be weighed one notable failure. In the autumn of 1775 the Americans sent an expedition to Canada, hoping to bring that area into the Revolution on their side. By the spring of 1776 it was clear that this expedition had failed. Though the failure was both military and political, Americans reassured one another that no such thing could occur among themselves. If the Canadians lacked the noble urge to be free, if they would not help themselves, then they deserved slavery. Meanwhile American patriots would establish their rights on battlefields closer to home.

The assurance of the Americans was ultimately justified by events: they did win, and their greatest asset was, in fact, their desire to be free. Though this desire did not enable them to maintain in the field a force equal to that of the British, the American armies could always count on popular support. It is true that many Americans took the British side—the best current estimate is that they amounted to a fifth of the population. Many of them shared the view that England had violated colonial rights, but they did not think the violations insufferable, and they turned out in substantial numbers to help the British troops keep the colonies in the empire. Nowhere, however, were they strong enough to enable royal government to survive. At the beginning of the war all the royal governors fled, and only in Georgia, the least populous of the revolting colonies, was British civil government re-established during the remainder of the war.

A large portion of the population may have been indifferent at the outset, content to stay British if the British won or to go along with independence if the patriots could make it stick. But the war itself sooner or later obliged men to get off the fence on one side or the other. The independent state governments called on their people for military service again and again, for a tour of duty in either the militia or the Continental Army. When the call came, a man had to shoulder a musket in the cause or else abandon home and family and head for the British lines. Most preferred to go along with their countrymen; and once they had spent some months in camp, perhaps shooting at the British and being shot at by them, they were likely to return committed to the Revolution.

The Revolution, in other words, became a people's war, and it is doubtful that the British could ever have won more than a stalemate. They might defeat the American forces in the field, as they often did, but victory did not enable them to occupy the country without a much larger force than they ever had. Americans generally owned guns and knew how to use them. A century and a half of defending themselves against French and Indians, the reliance many placed on guns to protect their crops from animals and to provide themselves with meat—these had given them a familiarity with firearms that common people of the Old World lacked. It was this experience that told at Concord and at Bunker Hill. And it would tell again whenever a British army attempted to sweep through the country. Men would gather from the farms, snipe at the troops, ambush them, raid them, until the victory parade turned into a hasty retreat.

This great asset, which made a British victory most unlikely, unfortunately did not insure an American victory. The local militia were good at harassing the British, but they were the least reliable part of the American forces when it came to pitched battles, and they could never be kept in the field for more than a short time. As soon as a battle was over, sometimes before, they would be on their way home. It took something more than a militia to make the war end in American victory.

How much more it took began to be apparent very soon after Congress took the plunge to independence. On July 2, while the members were adopting their resolution, General William Howe was landing unopposed on Staten Island in New York with several thousand troops. Shortly afterward his brother, Admiral Lord

Howe, arrived with a battle fleet, and during the rest of the summer men and supplies poured in until there were more than thirty thousand men in arms on the island. Along with this force the Howes bore a commission enabling them to offer pardon to all Americans, provided they submitted to the authority of King and Parliament. The offer was laughable at this stage, but the force accompanying it was not.

Washington was on hand to oppose the expected attack and had almost as many men available as Howe, but most of them were militia. Washington himself had had a good deal less experience in command than his opponent, and in the ensuing Battle of Long Island (August 26, 1776) he was badly beaten and only saved from losing most of his forces by good luck and by Howe's failure to take full advantage of opportunities. There followed a humiliating series of defeats in which Washington and his army were chased across New Jersey.

There now began to appear, however, two factors which were to weigh heavily in determining the outcome of the war. One was the mediocrity of the commanders England sent to subdue the colonists. It is always difficult to determine in advance whether a field commander will be up to his job—so much depends on chance and on making the right decision at precisely the right moment. There were doubtless men among the British officers in America who might have succeeded in crushing Washington and destroying his army in 1776; but General Howe was a cautious, methodical soldier, not given to taking chances. He pursued war by the rulebook, and though capable of brilliant planning he was not good at seizing unexpected opportunities. After pushing Washington across the Delaware River by December, he called a halt for the winter.

Washington and his subordinates meanwhile were learning

about war the hard way. The fact that he and they had the talent to learn was a second factor working toward American success. In spite of numerous defeats and in spite of the vanishing militia, Washington still had the remnants of an army. When he found that the British were disposed to halt for the winter, he turned and hit them hard. On the famous night of December 25, 1776, he recrossed the Delaware and with very little loss to his own men captured 1,000 Hessians under Colonel Rall at Trenton. It was not a battle of great importance in itself, but it showed which commander had the daring and the initiative to win a war, and it restored to the Americans some of the assurance they had begun to lose.

In the following year General Howe along with his subordinate, General Burgoyne, gave the Americans further reason for confidence. With Howe's approval Burgoyne conducted an expedition from Canada down the Hudson Valley to cut off New England from the other colonies. This was the old French strategy, and since the British already held New York, it would have been a simple matter to send a column up from New York to meet the other coming down from Canada. But instead of sending such a column from New York, Howe moved the main body of his troops to Philadelphia. Washington, baffled as he well might be by what Howe was doing, tried to bar the way, but the British troops swept triumphantly into the city. There was probably no city in America that Howe could not have taken with the force at his disposal. Neither did he gain much by his entry—most Americans did not live in Philadelphia.

And while Howe was receiving the encomiums of Pennsylvania loyalists, the farmers of New England and New York were giving Burgoyne a bad time in the Hudson Valley. He had made his march from Canada to the accompaniment of manifestos calling upon the people to come in and be saved from the awful tyranny of the

Revolution. They came in, but not to be saved, and Continental troops came in too. On October 17, 1777, at Saratoga, Burgoyne surrendered to them.

He surrendered not only the tattered remains of his forces but also much of the prestige which for Europeans still clung to British arms. Saratoga was a great turning point of the war, because it won for Americans the foreign assistance which was the last element needed for victory. The possibility of such assistance had played an important role in their calculations from the beginning. The Declaration of Independence itself was issued mainly for the purpose of assuring potential allies that Americans were playing for keeps and would not fly into the mother country's arms at the first sign of parental indulgence.

Among possible allies the most likely had always been France. Ever since the peace of 1763 she had been waiting for opportunities of revenge against Britain and observing the alienation of the colonies with growing satisfaction. On May 2, 1776, two months before the Americans declared themselves independent, before they had even asked for aid, Louis XVI, on the advice of his foreign minister Vergennes, made a million livres (about $185,000 or £41,666 sterling) available to them for the purchase of munitions. And Vergennes persuaded Spain to put up an equal amount. The money and supplies which reached America from Europe were of the utmost importance. The money, of which there was much more to come both in gifts and loans, bolstered the credit of the United States and made it possible to finance the war. The munitions were indispensable because America, not yet an industrial country, could scarcely produce what she needed in sufficient quantities.

But money and supplies furnished secretly were different from outright military and naval assistance. France had been ready to give the one before she was asked; the other she was much slower to risk. Congress sent Benjamin Franklin to seek it, and if anyone could have got it by sheer persuasiveness, he could have. The French lionized him, pampered him, quoted him, but Vergennes retired behind his diplomatic fences and waited to see how much staying power the Americans would show. The Frenchman knew what a beating Washington had taken on Long Island, and he did not wish to expose France to a war with Great Britain unless the Americans could carry a real share of the burden. Vergennes was still waiting—and so was Franklin—when news of Saratoga arrived.

It was now Vergennes' turn to move. Saratoga demonstrated that the Americans could force the surrender of a British army. It seemed likely now that with French help they could win. Even England seemed to have reached that conclusion, for a commission under the Earl of Carlisle was directed to offer them everything they had asked for short of independence. Reconciliation was the last thing Vergennes wished to see, and Franklin exploited his fear of it to win the greatest diplomatic victory the United States has ever achieved. In February, 1778, France signed two treaties, one of Amity and Commerce in which she recognized the United States and the two countries agreed to help each other commercially, the other of Alliance. This second treaty (on which Vergennes now insisted) gave the Americans all they could have hoped for and exacted almost nothing in return. It was to go into effect in case war should break out between England and France—as it did the following June (1778)—and it stated specifically that its essential purpose was to maintain the ''liberty, sovereignty, and independence absolute and unlimited of the United States.'' France renounced all future possession of the Bermuda Islands and of any part of North America east of the Mississippi. If the United States conquered Canada or the Bermudas in the course of the war, France would recognize them as part of the United States. The two parties agreed to make no separate peace with Great Britain, and neither was to lay down arms until the independence of the United States was assured. For all this, France required only a recognition by the United States of whatever conquests she should make in the West Indies.

Vergennes tried hard but unsuccessfully to get Spain to join the alliance. The Spaniards were as much against Great Britain as the French, but they did not like the idea of recognizing revolted colonies—they had too many of their own which might be encouraged to follow America's example. Nevertheless, the Spaniards could not long resist the opportunity to strike at Britain. With an eye on Gibraltar they entered the war in June, 1779, as an ally of France though not of the United States.

With France and Spain in the war the materials for an American victory were assembled. England would now have to fight on several fronts and keep a large number of troops and ships at home to protect herself against possible invasion. Moreover, France sent both men and ships to assist the Americans directly, six thousand soldiers under the Comte de Rochambeau and a fleet of seventeen vessels under the Comte d'Estaing and later another of twenty-eight vessels under Admiral de Grasse. The ships were particularly welcome because the Americans, though well equipped with privateers, had virtually no navy.

It nevertheless took more than three painful years after the French entrance into the war for Washington to find the opportunity for a decisive battle. After Saratoga, General Howe submitted his resignation and was replaced by General Henry Clinton, who had orders to shift the scene of the British offensive to the South and pursue a policy of attrition in the North. As the French naval force was not large enough to aspire to superiority in the Atlantic, D'Estaing occupied himself mostly in the Caribbean. Clinton consequently was able to subject the American coastal towns to heavy raids and at the same time to mount an offensive against Georgia and South Carolina. Clinton was a more energetic commander than Howe. During 1779 he recovered Georgia, and by May, 1780, had taken Charleston, South Carolina, and its garrison of five thousand men. Leaving Cornwallis in command of an army of eight thousand to continue the southern campaign, he departed for the North to take care of a French expedition against Newport, Rhode Island, which the British had occupied since 1776.

Cornwallis, continuing to move northward with greater haste than Clinton had anticipated, was initially successful and inflicted another crushing defeat on the Americans at Camden, South Carolina (August 16, 1780). But as he pressed on through the interior, the presence of a hostile, armed population began to make itself felt. And in December, 1780, Washington sent General Nathanael Greene, perhaps his ablest subordinate, to concert the American resistance. Greene struck at Cornwallis in a damaging series of quick, sharp jabs, relying on speedy attack and withdrawal to prevent his opponent from using his full force. Rather than retreat, Cornwallis pressed on to Virginia in 1781, while Greene shifted his raiding farther south, where he not only prevented the British from coming to the relief of Cornwallis but made them fight hard to retain the coastal cities of Savannah and Charleston.

As a result Washington had the chance to isolate Cornwallis. With the aid of French forces exceeding the American by two to one, he closed in on Yorktown from land and sea simultaneously. The French fleet under De Grasse achieved temporary superiority in the area; the French and American soldiers outnumbered the

British, and together they forced Cornwallis to surrender his entire army (which still amounted to more than seven thousand men) on October 17, 1781.

When the news reached England, everyone but George III knew that the war was over. Lord North had been trying to resign ever since Saratoga, but the King held doggedly on, and though no further campaigns were undertaken against the Americans, British forces continued to hammer at the French and Spanish in other parts of the world for another year—and not without success. During that time American, French, Spanish, and British diplomats were scurrying back and forth across the English Channel with proposals and counterproposals both open and secret. The big question was what boundaries the United States should have. Spain would gladly have seen the Americans cooped up east of the Appalachians. France too, having humbled Britain, was not eager to raise a colossus in the New World and was less than enthusiastic in pressing American claims for territory.

The American peace commissioners, Franklin, John Jay, and John Adams, were instructed by Congress to insist only on independence and to follow the advice of the French in everything else; but they took the liberty of violating their instructions by negotiating what amounted to a separate peace (which Vergennes, however, accepted gracefully). By so doing they won for the United States in the final treaty (September 3, 1783) a northern boundary that still holds, a western boundary at the Mississippi, and a southern boundary at the thirty-first parallel. They did not get Canada, and they did not get the right to trade freely in British ports, both of which Franklin had argued for with some hope of success, but what they got was space enough for the Americans to prove themselves and their principles.

VII

The Independent States

When the world was told on July 4, 1776, that "these United Colonies are, and of right ought to be Free and Independent States," not even the members of the Continental Congress knew precisely what they had done. The ties that formerly bound them to Great Britain were cut. What was left? "Nothing," said a few, who saw themselves in the "state of nature." If they were right, then everything would have to be rebuilt from the ground up: territorial boundaries, schools, business companies, law courts, churches, towns—all would be reduced to nothing; all would have to be reconstructed.

Most Americans thought nothing so drastic was needed. In a few years they would look on in mingled admiration and horror while the people of France reduced themselves to such a state of nature, but among themselves there was little urge to rebuild society. Though they had committed themselves to the principle of human equality, most of them applied it only in equating themselves with Englishmen and did not stop to examine whatever inequities might exist in their relations with each other. The important thing was not to reform society but to keep government subordinate to it. There was no reason, they thought, why a government which had got out of hand might not be replaced by a proper one without destroying the social fabric for which government should form a protective coating. One could simply peel off the old government and put on the new.

John Locke himself, the great authority on the subject, had never claimed that the dissolution of government would throw a people back into the state of nature. He in fact emphasized that society came into existence before government and could survive a change of government, as English society had done in 1688. If England could do it in 1688, America could do it in 1776.

Since these ideas prevailed among the majority, the change from British to American government was made with very little fuss. After Lexington the royal governors fled back to England without waiting for the Declaration of Independence. Provincial congresses, in most cases almost indistinguishable from the old assemblies, assumed provisional control of their respective areas. The Continental Congress in May, 1776, advised the people to set up regular governments on their own authority, and by July 4 they had already begun to do so.

In constructing these new governments the ex-colonists did not forget the century and a half during which they had lived in contentment under British rule. They still possessed an admiration for the British constitution that was only slightly tarnished by their recent experiences. Until their final repudiation of the King they had insisted that they were contending only for what the constitution required. They still believed that it was they who stayed true to it while King and Parliament betrayed it. The fact nevertheless remained that it had been betrayed: for all its excellence it had not been proof against tyranny. The problem was to design a government containing all the virtues of the British constitution but with added safeguards to prevent the kind of deterioration they had just witnessed.

There were actually two kinds of government to build, central and local. They began discussing the central one, as we shall see, even before declaring independence but were unable to finish it for several years. In forming the local state governments they were more successful: ten were completed by the end of 1776 and the rest by 1780. They were not perfect, but they did furnish greater protection to human liberty than could be found in any other part of the world at the time.

The most striking thing about these state governments is that they all had their wings clipped by written constitutions in which their powers were strictly limited and defined. In Rhode Island and Connecticut the old colonial charters continued to serve this purpose, but in each of the other states a special document was drafted. The British constitution was unwritten, and in the recent dispute each side had pelted the other with historical precedents. Though the colonists gave as good as they got in this fracas, they had had enough of it and were now unanimous in feeling that their new governments should have something more than tradition to limit and guide them.

A written constitution, then, was their first line of defense against tyranny, and it generally contained a bill of rights defining certain liberties of the people which government must not invade under any pretext: general warrants and standing armies were forbidden; freedom of the press, the right to petition, trial by jury, habeas corpus, and other procedures that came to be known as "due process of law" were guaranteed.

In their haste to get a properly limited government in operation most states allowed their provincial congresses to assume the task of drafting a constitution and putting it into effect. The people of

The Independent States

Massachusetts seem to have been the first to see the danger of this procedure. When their provisional legislature handed them a constitution in 1778, they refused the gift, not merely because they did not like it, but also because they had decided that the people should endow the government with a constitution and not vice versa. If, they reasoned, a government can make its own constitution, the government can change it and thus fall into tyranny. Accordingly a special convention was held in 1780 and a constitution established by the people acting independently of government. Other Americans, equally concerned with the dangers of usurpation, saw at once the desirability of the Massachusetts procedure. Though by this time it was too late for most states to use it, the new method was shortly followed in creating a government for the United States.

Though drafted by provincial congresses rather than popular conventions, the state constitutions did nevertheless proceed on the assumption that the people are the source of political power. Virginia, the first to complete one, began it with a bill of rights which asserted that "all power is vested in, and consequently derived from, the people; that magistrates are their trustees and servants, and at all times amenable to them." Other states copied this provision and supported it by various devices to prevent their governments from slipping the reins of popular control.

It was of elementary importance that every officer of government be elected directly or indirectly by the people. There must be no office of hereditary right, no king, no house of lords. Some constitutions made express provisions to this effect; others simply specified the term of every office, usually a year except in the case of judges. But even though the new governors and judges were to be elective, there remained a much greater confidence in the legislative branch of government than in the executive or judiciary. The members of the legislature, it was felt, were more intimately

90

connected with the people and more immediately subject to them. The governor was generally not allowed to veto legislative acts. He could not dissolve or prorogue legislative meetings. In many states he was elected by the legislature and could be impeached by it. The colonial assemblies had whittled away at the powers of the royal governors for a century and a half, and when the opportunity came could not resist the temptation to finish the job. Pennsylvania decided that a governor was only a nuisance anyhow and abolished the office altogether; in most other states it might as well have been abolished.

John Adams, the Braintree lawyer who helped the Massachusetts Assembly reject the authority of Parliament, saw that the states were making their executive departments too weak. Now that the governor represented popular rather than royal authority, it would have been safer to give him enough power to check an overambitious legislature. Adams was unable to persuade his countrymen of this, but he was successful in urging another device for limiting the legislature, namely, to split it into two chambers, each of which must agree to every act.

Because America had no titled aristocracy and did not want one, it seemed to many, including Benjamin Franklin, that American legislatures should be unicameral, with no upper house. Adams, however, was convinced that an upper house was more than a sanctuary for pampered aristocrats. It was a vantage point from which men of property might slow down the more extravagant schemes of a thoughtless multitude. It was also a place where ambitious men of great prestige might be safely and happily isolated without endangering the liberties of the masses. Though America might grant no titles of nobility, Adams was convinced that every society grows aristocrats as inevitably as a field of corn will grow some large ears and some small. Whether by wealth, birth, or

The Independent States

talents, some individuals would gain an influence over the others; the function of the upper house was to furnish a place where their influence might be restrained within defined limits.

Adams was not very clear about the way these natural aristocrats were to be prevented from infiltrating the lower house too, but by letters to influential friends and by a well-timed pamphlet he did succeed in persuading every state except Pennsylvania to make its new legislature bicameral. Since most colonial assemblies had contained an upper house in the form of the Governor's Council, it was easy enough to continue the institution on an elective basis.

While they carried out in these institutions the principle that all power emanates from the people, the constitutions were less consistent in applying another principle which most of them enunciated: that all men were born free and equal. Though power emanated from the people, it did not emanate from all of them equally. Western areas in the colonies from Pennsylvania southward had not enjoyed under royal government a representation in proportion to their population, and in the new governments they still had less than their share. There were also people, varying in number from state to state, from whom no power emanated at all, because they did not have enough property to vote or because they belonged to the wrong sex or the wrong race.

That the toleration of these inequalities was inconsistent with the avowed principles of the Revolution did not escape men at the time, and the Revolutionary period did see a general reduction in property requirements for voting and an increase in western representation. In some states, notably Pennsylvania, there was a thorough electoral reform that secured all taxpayers the right to vote and provided for keeping representation in harmony with population by periodic reapportionments. In other states there were similar though incomplete reforms, and in still others there had never been either regional inequalities in representation or disbarment of large numbers of adult males from the suffrage. In no state was representation reduced, and only in Massachusetts was the property qualification increased, and there only slightly.

In failing to establish proportional representation and universal suffrage, the Revolutionists showed that they were not prepared to follow the principle of equality to its logical political conclusion even for adult white men. We need not, however, conclude that their enunciation of the principle was hypocrisy. Though we still adhere to it and though we have carried it farther than our ancestors, we are still finding new applications. During the Revolutionary period the men who formulated it could scarcely begin to know where it might take them.

Their reluctance to extend political equality to men without property must be seen in the context of the ideas that had guided their resistance to England. The Revolution had begun as a dispute over the security of property, and had fed on the conviction that government existed for the protection of property. It followed that men who had no property must be less concerned with government than those who did. Moreover, Harrington had shown that if men who owned no property to support their independence had a share in government, they would be unable to resist the coercion of tyrants or the blandishments of political adventurers, would-be tyrants eager to buy their votes with bread and circuses. Harrington's contention that a wide, generally equal distribution of property was the best safeguard of a free government had led his followers so far as to proclaim that "equality [meaning economic equality] is the soul of liberty." But they had not envisioned a total equality. And neither, to begin with at least, did the Americans.

Their original intention had been merely to affirm their equality with Englishmen. When they called upon Locke's philosophy of government to support the affirmation, they did not perceive that they were opening the door to developments that Locke himself would probably have disavowed. Locke had described the state of nature as a state of perfect equality, in which no man enjoyed any kind of right or authority or dignity beyond another. In so doing he had no intention of unseating English dukes and earls from their exalted position in the settled state of English society. Locke's state of nature was purely hypothetical, and he did not suggest that the equality prevailing in it ought to continue in organized society. Nor did the revolution he was defending bring about any upset in the social structure of England.

Most Americans, as we have seen, thought of their revolution in much the same way: they too were beyond the hypothetical state of nature and need not return to it. But in America there was not as wide a gap as in England between the hypothetical state of nature and the actual state of society. Here were no titled nobility and no degraded peasantry. Most people owned land and enjoyed economic independence. They were more nearly equal than the people of any European country, and with the wilderness beckoning on the other side of the mountains they could easily picture the state of nature as a real thing. Under these circumstances Locke's description of the perfect equality of natural men gradually became an ideal to be preserved in American society. Though there was no radical rebuilding of social institutions at this time, it is nevertheless possible to see the ideal beginning to take shape and operating, if only fitfully, against the grosser social inequalities of the day.

The grossest, of course, was slavery. America had been a land of opportunity for white men, who had come by the thousands to enjoy the benefits of the land that any enterprising free man could acquire. But in the South the blessings of liberty had grown side-by-side with the burdens of slavery, and the two were locked in an embrace not easily broken. In Virginia slaves made up 41 per cent of the population, in North Carolina 34 per cent, in South Carolina 53 per cent, in Georgia 37 per cent. The opportunities that had brought economic independence and the corresponding political rights to white men in these states might have been considerably reduced if so large a proportion of the population had not been permanently engaged in improving the condition of white men. To free the slaves at a stroke would have meant not only to impoverish their owners but to invite anarchy. Or so at least it seemed to most southerners. "If you free the slaves," said Landon Carter, who owned several hundred, "you must send them out of the country or they must steal for their support."

The Revolutionists nevertheless were uneasy about the liberty and labor that they themselves, in effect, had stolen from their slaves. Early in the agitation against Great Britain, individuals had remarked on the inconsistency of a people holding slaves and at the same time complaining that Parliamentary taxation would reduce them to slavery. As the struggle progressed, more and more Americans came to see the need for casting out this beam. In July, 1774, Rhode Island led the way with a law providing that all slaves imported thereafter should be freed. That the move was prompted by the new equalitarian ideas is evident from the preamble, which states that "those who are desirous of enjoying all the advantages of liberty themselves should be willing to extend personal liberty to others." Under this same impulse the Continental Congress in 1774 agreed to discontinue the slave trade and to boycott those who engaged in it. Connecticut, Delaware, Virginia, Maryland, South Carolina, and North Carolina passed laws in the 1770's and 1780's either forbidding or discouraging the importation of slaves. Jefferson would have included a statement against slavery in the Declaration of Independence had not other members of congress ruled it out.

In most of the northern states the abolition of the slave trade was followed shortly by the abolition of slavery itself. The Massachusetts constitution of 1780 declared in its first article, "All men are born free and equal." Under this clause the courts found it necessary in several lawsuits to determine whether slavery was legal in Massachusetts. They ruled that it was not, and by 1790 Massachusetts could report that there were no slaves in the state. Other northern states provided by legislation for gradual abolition. Even the southern states, though they continued to hold slaves, admitted the injustice of doing so and looked for a way of abolishing the evil without bringing about their own economic ruin. They did not find a way, but so many southerners were conscience stricken by their own conduct that in 1782 the Virginia legislature passed a law permitting manumission. This had hitherto been forbidden, but now, in the next eight years, ten thousand Virginia slaves received their freedom by the voluntary action of owners who took the principle of equality literally.

The first assaults on slavery were matched by a more successful move toward equality in religion. In 1776 most colonies collected taxes for support of the ministry, and one church generally got the bulk of the funds, if not all of them, regardless of its size. In the southern colonies it was the Anglican church, in New England the Congregational. During the Revolution, partly because of pressure from other denominations, partly because of the new disposition toward equality, the Anglican church everywhere lost its special position, and most states left the churches of every denomination to support themselves by voluntary donation of their members. But the New England states continued their support, still favoring the

The Independent States

Congregationalists, in New Hampshire until 1817, in Connecticut until 1818, and in Massachusetts until 1833.

Besides the deliberate extension of equality to some slaves and churches, the Revolution brought in its train a host of incalculable accidental and incidental changes in society, many of which tended toward a redistribution of wealth. The war made new fortunes and ruined old ones. Among the heaviest losers were the merchants. Particularly during the early years of the fighting, their business was disrupted by the British Navy. Cut off from trade routes within the Empire, they were obliged to seek out new ones, and these seldom proved initially as profitable as the old. Many turned their ships to privateering against English vessels and occasionally struck it rich, but this required a special talent and was not nearly as reliable a source of income as regular commerce. Few of the established merchant firms of the colonial period came through the Revolution unscathed.

The big southern planters were also hard hit, for the war interfered with the marketing of their rice and tobacco. It was some time after peace arrived before they recovered, and in tidewater Virginia the great plantations never did regain the old grandeur.

On the other hand, many small farmers enjoyed a prosperity they had never known before. Armies marched on their stomachs in the American Revolution too, and the farmers who supplied them commanded unheard-of prices. With part of the population in the army, albeit a relatively small proportion, there was more work for the civilians and more profit.

The prosperity of the small man was heightened also by the inflation of the currency in every state. The Revolutionary governments, in spite of the fact that they claimed to be trustees of the people, were at first reluctant to impose the high taxes needed to finance the war, and the Continental Congress had no power to tax at all. Instead of taxes both Congress and the state governments resorted to printing money to supply their needs. The result was a flood of paper bills which sent prices soaring. In such a situation the farmer, who was frequently a debtor, could sell his crops at astronomical prices and pay off his debts at their face value in currency that was worth only a fraction of what it had been when he borrowed it.

The inflation of the currency together with the removal of British authority also made opportunities for speculators to amass fortunes. The role of these men in American history has generally been a dishonorable one, and this period no less than others had its shady characters and fast deals. But while he was making his pile, the speculator incidentally was helping his countrymen to a wider distribution of property. He thrived on the estates that were everywhere confiscated from those who opposed the Revolution and professed loyalty to Great Britain. These estates were sometimes very large, and through the speculators they were split and transferred to smaller buyers.

A further distribution of property was brought about by reform of inheritance laws. Hitherto in many states the eldest son of a man who died without a will would receive all his father's land; in some cases he might even be required to pass it on intact to his own eldest son. These customs, known as "primogeniture" and "entail," were originally designed to perpetuate an aristocracy. They were felt to be out of place in the new America and were everywhere abolished during the Revolutionary period.

The changes of these years, both social and political, were not accomplished without disagreements among the Revolutionists themselves. Some wanted to go much farther, others not this far. The disagreements have so impressed historians that the Revolution is sometimes interpreted as an internal struggle in

The Independent States

which the contest between different classes and parties looms as large as the conflict between England and America. Carl Becker, for example, in examining the origins of the Revolution in New York stated that it was not only a dispute about home rule but also about who should rule at home, and his aphorism has become the theme of many subsequent histories.

It cannot be denied that both disputes existed, but to magnify the internal contest to the same proportions as the revolt against England is to distort it beyond recognition. Both before and after the struggle Americans of every state were divided socially, sectionally, and politically; but these divisions did not with any consistency coincide with the division between patriot and loyalist, nor did they run so deep as to arouse the same intensity of feeling. The Revolution cut across the old lines and plucked loyalists and patriots alike from every class and section. And though an ardent patriotism was often used by one group or another to advance its own political fortunes, no group was able to monopolize the commodity. During the war (as before and after it), in spite of the many opportunities for violence, internal disputes generally found peaceable if noisy settlement within the ordinary framework of politics.

The most radical change produced in Americans by the Revolution was in fact not a division at all but the union of three million cantankerous colonists into a new nation.

VIII

The Independent Nation, 1776-81

Nationalism has been the great begetter of revolutions. In Europe, in Asia, in Africa, we have seen it stir one people after another: they grow proud of their traditions, of their language, of their identity, and they strike for independence. In our case it was the other way round: we struck for independence and were thereby stirred into nationality; our nation was the child, not the father, of our revolution.

We did, of course, have some of the makings of a nation before 1776. We spoke, for the most part, the same language; we enjoyed common historical traditions; we occupied a continuous territory; we were almost all Protestants. We had even developed a certain self-consciousness, a pride in things American. Nevertheless, it was not this pride that drove the colonists to resist British taxation. All the colonial demands might have been satisfied within the limits of empire, had there been any disposition in London to satisfy them. Only as they saw every other means fail did Americans turn to independence.

Once they turned, however, the view proved fair beyond belief, and the means inexorably became an end, a goal that encompassed all previous ones. Independence, once sighted, seemed one with

The Independent Nation, 1776–81

liberty and equality and inseparable from them—it is only the nationalism of other peoples that ever appears ugly or dangerous.

So American nationalism appeared to the British, who detected signs of it early in the dispute. It had been a commonplace that the colonies could not be kept forever, that sometime in the dim and—it was to be hoped—distant future they would attain independence. No one, least of all the Americans, wished the event to come in the eighteenth century, but the British feared it and by meeting every protest against Parliament as a step toward it eventually brought about the very thing they feared. The British efforts to curb a supposed drive toward independence united Americans in a common sense of grievance and alarm, nourishing a sense of togetherness that grew steadily toward nationality.

The process, we can see now, began at the time of the Stamp Act when the colonists surprised themselves not only by the unanimity of their opposition to the tax but also by their ability to agree to a declaration of principles at the Congress in New York. After the meeting was over and repeal was on the way, Joseph Warren of Massachusetts wrote enthuiastically to a friend that the Stamp Act had accomplished "what the most zealous Colonist never could have expected! The Colonies until now were ever at variance and foolishly jealous of each other, they are now . . . united . . . nor will they soon forget the weight which this close union gives them."

In the years that followed, each time the colonists felt obliged to use the weight of union, the closeness of union was strengthened, for with each new contest they were discovering a wider agreement in principle. When the time came to cut loose from the mother country and set up government for themselves, they were ready to build upon a common core of political beliefs. They believed that government must protect property and not take it in taxes without

101

consent, that government is the product of those who are governed by it and subject to alteration by them at any time. They knew that men are evil by nature and that governments are consequently prone to corruption. Together they watched the British government succumb to evil, and together they decided to do something about it.

By 1776 the consciousness that they belonged together had grown so strong that the phrase "United Colonies" had a singular as well as a plural meaning. When the Declaration of Independence substituted "States" for "Colonies," the singular meaning was still present, and it did not even occur to the colonists that they might establish thirteen separate governments and go their different ways. They must win independence together or not at all, and they must have some sort of central government to give expression to their existence as a nation.

Politicians argued for nearly a century over the question whether the national government was older or younger than the state governments. Historians still argue over it. But in 1776 Americans believed that the Declaration of Independence created the United States as well as the several states; and the Continental Congress which made the Declaration seemed as much a provisional government for the nation as the provincial congresses were for the states. The Declaration itself indicates as much when it says that "as Free and Independent States they have full power to levy war, conclude peace, contract alliances, establish commerce, and to do all other acts and things which independent States may of right do." Though given a plural wording, "Independent States" must have been intended to convey a singular as well as a plural meaning, for it was Congress, the central government of the nation, that levied war against Great Britain, contracted an alliance with France, and concluded peace.

The Independent Nation, 1776-81

When the members of the Continental Congress began to consider a declaration that would turn the United Colonies into the United States, they immediately took steps to prepare a constitution so that the new nation, as soon as it should be born, could be clothed in a properly defined and limited government. On June 12, 1776, a committee was appointed to draft such a document. Like most committees, it did not move as fast as history and was not able to report until a month later, after independence had already been declared. What it then proposed (in a report drafted by John Dickinson) was a formalization of the existing situation, with all the functions of the central government assigned to a congress composed of delegates annually appointed by the several states. The congress was to have exclusive authority over some matters and concurrent authority with the states over others, but there was very little indication of how it was to put its decisions into effect.

When the members of the existing Congress began to debate the Dickinson report, they soon found out that the forming of a national government posed problems which the previous history of America did not equip them to surmount. Most of them had had abundant political experience in local assemblies, but none of them had participated in the imperial administration—if they had, perhaps there would have been no revolution. Though they were rapidly learning the art of dealing with a continent rather than a colony, they had been at it for less than two years, during which their efforts had been directed exclusively toward opposing the British. Now when they were required to define the relations of the states to each other and to the nation, all the old divisive forces—the local quarrels and jealousies that had divided the colonies before 1763—reasserted themselves. To make matters worse, Congress discovered that it had inherited some of the hostility generated against imperial control during the preceding decade. Just as Americans continued to be suspicious of governors even when they were elective, so they continued to be suspicious of central authority even when it was their own.

During the summer of 1776 these obstacles blocked the efforts of Congress to work out the details of the proposed constitution. The members could not agree on an equitable way of apportioning either expenses or voting, and there were conflicting opinions about what should be done with the western territories to which some states laid claim. While they argued, the members had also to give their attention to the approaching Battle of Long Island and to the hundred other problems of conducting a government that was already in existence even though it had not been properly created. As these problems mounted, they temporarily put aside their constitution-making and got on with the business of defeating Great Britain, arbitrarily assuming the powers they needed to get the job done.

They were aware, however, that they must tread lightly lest they inadvertently encourage the lingering suspicion of central government and dampen the national enthusiasm that was necessary to sustain the war effort. They did not, for instance, venture to impose taxes, because, having been chosen by state legislatures or provincial congresses rather than by direct vote, they were not in the fullest sense representatives of the people. Yet they could not run a war without money, and so they turned to a method which they had devised as colonists for mortgaging their future: they assumed the authority to issue bills of credit (in other words, paper money). In this way they hoped to translate national enthusiasm into concrete economic support.

Paper money worked well at first, and the war could scarcely have been fought without it. But as time passed and the fighting dragged on, Congress learned what many governments have found to their sorrow before and since, that patriotism is more readily transformed into blood and death than it is into dollars and cents. Merchants and farmers did not have enough faith in the credit of the nation to accept its paper money at face value. Every month saw the bills worth less. In September, 1779, Congress tried to halt the fall by resolving to issue no more, but as the bills continued to decline anyhow, in March, 1780, it reversed its decision and put the presses to work again. By the following spring the bills were costing more to print than they were worth.

It was at this point, with the only independent source of income exhausted, that the United States at last acquired a constitution— though not one which would do much to bolster its credit. When Congress had resumed discussion of the proposed constitution in April, 1777, the claims of the particular states were heard on its floors in a swelling chorus from men who often looked upon themselves more as watchdogs of local interests than as participants in a larger enterprise. Such a man, for example, was Dr. Thomas Burke, congressman from North Carolina. Burke thought he discerned in the central government a grasping for power of the kind that signalled a degeneration into tyranny. Rather than risk erecting another tyranny in place of the one just destroyed, he favored dissolving Congress altogether as soon as the war should be won. National feeling was too strong to allow serious consideration of such a proposal, but Burke was able to win adoption of a strong states' rights clause which found its way into the finished constitution as Article 2: "Each State retains its sovereignty, freedom and independence, and every power, jurisdiction, and right, which is not by this confederation expressly delegated to the United States, in Congress assembled."

Esteem for the state governments and a corresponding distrust of the central government was rising all over the country. While the latter was losing its credit in the avalanche of paper, the states were able to begin the climb into comparative solvency by levying taxes. Most of them had constitutions by 1777, and as Congress groped its way down the uncharted path of national government, the state governments were entrenching themselves behind a growing body of legislation. They were in fact so jealous of their new strength that when Congress finally finished tinkering with the constitution on November 17, 1777, and presented it to them, they were not at all eager to ratify it.

It is true that the Articles of Confederation, as the document was called, assigned what appeared to be a formidable list of powers to the Congress, which remained the only department in the central government. Congress was to have exclusive authority over relations with foreign countries, including the determination of war and peace, over admiralty cases, over disputes between different states, over coining money and establishing weights and measures, over trade with the Indians outside the boundaries of particular states, and over postal communications. In addition, it was authorized to borrow money and to requisition the states for men and money. Decisions were to be made by a simple majority, with each state having one vote, except in specified important matters for which the consent of at least nine states was necessary.

Though these powers when set forth in black and white looked imposing, they hardly merited any alarm over states' rights or popular liberty; for they were actually no more than Congress had been exercising on a *de facto* basis since independence, and the states had nevertheless grown steadily stronger and popular liberties more extensive. Furthermore, the Articles carefully safeguarded the states against encroachment from the central government by leaving to them the power of the purse. Congress could requisition them for money, but if they refused, the Articles provided no means to enforce the demand or for that matter to enforce any congressional decision. Their own experience in thwarting colonial governors might have reassured the American people that with the power of the purse the states were also retaining the ultimate power of government. They were also guarded against each other: equal voting by states was intended to protect the small states from the large and the nine-state majority to protect the large from the small.

But in spite of all its safeguards the people who had to judge this constitution could not at first bring themselves to ratify it. They were conditioned by the preceding ten or twelve years to approach all government with caution. In Massachusetts and New Hampshire they went over the Articles clause by clause in town meetings while local sages pointed out defects and dangers. Elsewhere the state legislatures talked it up and down much as Congress had already done and sent in recommendations for amendment, mostly designed to limit further the powers assigned the central government.

In only one important respect were these powers considered insufficient. The states without western land claims, particularly Maryland and New Jersey, felt that Congress should have the authority originally assigned it by the Dickinson committee to limit those states (Georgia, the Carolinas, Virginia, Connecticut, and Massachusetts) whose charters had named the Pacific Ocean as a western boundary. The lands beyond the settled regions, it was urged, would be won by the joint efforts of all the states in the Continental Army. What was thus purchased by the blood of all should belong to all.

The people of Maryland and New Jersey feared that unless the United States took over the western lands, the states that claimed them would have an immeasurable economic and political advantage over the others. Through sale of these lands the government, say of Virginia, might enjoy a steady income without taxing her citizens at all. As a result people would move from Maryland to Virginia to avoid taxes and would thus increase further the tax burden of those who were left behind, until Maryland and the other landless states would be depopulated and bankrupt. Better that all states be put on an equal footing and the western lands be given to the United States.

In evoking the philosophy of equality the landless states were of course seeking to further their own interests, just as Americans had been seeking to further their own interests in resisting British taxation, and the dissenting churches in seeking to end the special favors shown to the Anglicans and Congregationalists. The arguments for a cession of western lands were not less cogent because those who offered them stood to benefit. It must be pointed out, however, that much of the support came from a group of men who stood to gain privately far more then they disclosed, far more than an equality of the states.

These men were land speculators who had formed companies to develop the territory in question. The Illinois-Wabash Company and the Indiana Company, with a membership drawn largely from Pennsylvania, Maryland, and New Jersey, had made purchases from the Indians in the Ohio Valley before independence and were now seeking a governmental validation of their titles. They knew that Virginia held the best claim to the lands: as the first colony to be founded her claim antedated all others, and it covered most of the Mississippi Valley north of the Carolinas. But Virginia made it plain that she did not intend to recognize Indian purchases made by outsiders; she had speculators of her own to please. If, however, the lands were ceded to the United States, the members of the Indiana and Wabash companies hoped that congressmen would prove more pliant than the Virginia legislators. There was good reason to hope too, because many influential congressmen already held shares of stock in the companies and showed a more than charitable disposition toward them.

The speculators and their propagandists worked hard for a revision of the Articles of Confederation to give Congress control of the area where their investments lay. Not only did they argue that conquest of the West by the Continental armies would entitle the nation to sovereignty over it, but they also maintained that since the West had formerly belonged to Great Britain it should now belong to Congress, because, as they claimed, the authority of Great Britain had devolved upon Congress. The speculators were most influential in Maryland, and to enforce their arguments persuaded her not to ratify the Articles of Confederation unless amended to make the unbounded states give up their western lands.

Because of the urgency of union the other states agreed by early 1779 to ratify the basic document first and tackle the multitude of proposed amendments afterward. But Maryland held out. It is to the credit of the Virginians in this crisis that many of them recognized the validity of the principle Maryland was contending for, even while they called attention to the ulterior motives at work. And it is doubly fortunate that they discovered reasons closer to their own states' interests to justify limiting her size. There was a common assumption at this time that a republic could not cover more than a small territory and remain a republic. It was hoped that a confederation of republics might extend more widely, but a single republic, if spread too large, would prove weak and either fall prey to monarchical despotism or disintegrate into anarchy. Thomas Jefferson and Richard Henry Lee, both of whom expressed these views, thought that Virginia should voluntarily limit her size. Thus through an attachment to the principles of republican government they reached much the same position that men with other reasons had been contending for.

Because of these views and also because the British armies were now pressing up from the Carolinas, making the need of confederation seem daily more desperate, the Virginians agreed on January 2, 1781, to cede their territory north and west of the Ohio. In doing so, however, they stipulated certain conditions that carried much further the principle of equality upon which Maryland had insisted. Maryland had been worried about her own inferiority to so huge a sister state. Virginia was concerned about the future of the United States and of the people who should live in the territory she was resigning. She gave it up only on condition that it be held as a common fund for the nation—thus providing the United States with a national domain—and on condition also that it be laid out in separate new states not more than 150 and not less than 100 miles square, to be admitted eventually to the union with the same "rights of sovereignty, freedom, and independence as the other States." Virginia by her cession cut herself down to a size more nearly that of her sister states and gave all Americans an equal share in the possession of the West. At the same time, she guaranteed that future westerners should not become second-class citizens, that the United States should remain a union of equals without subordinate colonies of the British type.

Though Congress could not refuse these conditions, there was trouble over another of Virginia's stipulations, namely, that all Indian purchases in the area be declared void. The powerful land speculators were able to cause a shameful wrangle over this question, which delayed the acceptance of Virginia's offer for several years. It was apparent, however, that the land would ultimately belong to the United States. Maryland was thus left with no grounds on which she could conscientiously refrain from joining in the Articles of Confederation. But, still in the clutch of the land companies, she continued to delay. At this point she received a strong nudge—it might be called a kick—from the French Ambassador, La Luzerne, to whom she had appealed for the protection of French naval forces against British raids in the Chesapeake. The Ambassador, exceeding his powers, suggested that naval aid would not be forthcoming unless Maryland ratified the Articles. In February, 1781, she did so, and on March 1 the Confederation was formally announced.

IX

"The Critical Period"

81 – 9

The period during which the United States was governed under the Articles of Confederation, from 1781 to 1789, used to be considered a dark and doubtful time. A hundred years after it was over the historian John Fiske dubbed it "the critical period." Though the name has stuck, more recent historians have found much to praise in this critical period, so much that they have accused the politicians who ended it of acting for dubious, not to say sinister, motives. And indeed any serious student must acknowledge that under the Articles of Confederation the achievements of the United States were impressive. When the Articles were adopted, the country was at war for its existence. When they were abandoned, the war had been won, peace had been concluded on favorable terms, a postwar depression had been weathered successfully, and both population and national income were increasing.

Viewed in detail, the achievements are even more impressive, though marred by some sordid episodes. We have already seen how land speculation and republican principles combined to make a national domain possible. In March, 1784, when the long anticipated acquisition of the Northwest (the area north of the Ohio, west of Pennsylvania, and east of the Mississippi) by Congress at last became fact, the members lost no time in arranging for its government and settlement. On April 23, 1784, an ordinance, drafted principally by Thomas Jefferson but reflecting previous Congressional discussion of the subject, carved the territory into seven districts (with provision for more to the south when the Southwest should be ceded). Each was to be admitted to the union as a state on equal terms with the original thirteen as soon as it had as many free inhabitants as the smallest of them. Meanwhile, in each district the settlers were to govern themselves temporarily according to the constitution and laws of any one of the existing states, but were forbidden to interfere with any arrangements made by Congress for the sale of public lands. Such arrrangements were made in a second ordinance, passed in 1785, which provided for the survey and sale of these lands in townships six miles square, the lines running north-south and east-west. Each township was to contain thirty-six lots a mile square in area (640 acres), to be sold for not less than one dollar an acre.

The surveying was started as soon as the ordinance was passed, but before sales could get under way or government be organized, speculation entered the picture again. By a deal with corrupt congressmen a group of New Englanders, organized as the Ohio Company, bought a million and a half unsurveyed acres at a price that amounted to less than ten cents an acre in hard money. Congress was ready to consent to so drastic a discount not merely because influential congressmen were cut in on the bargain but also because the Northwest was filling up with settlers who showed no disposition to buy land at all. Without waiting for Indian treaties or surveys or sales, men who carried long rifles and an easy conscience were crossing the Ohio and setting up shacks and cabins on the land from which Congress hoped to pay its debts. Some of them even claimed a natural right to the land and denied that Congress had the authority to keep them off or to sell it at all.

In order to protect the only domain the United States could

claim as a nation, Congress was ready not only to sell at bargain prices to bona fide purchasers like the Ohio Company but also to take a more active role than it originally had intended in organizing government in the area. The Ohio Company, which hoped to attract large numbers of law-abiding New Englanders to the region, gladly cooperated in drafting a new ordinance for government of the territory. This "Northwest Ordinance," of July 13, 1787, instead of letting the settlers immediately select and operate their own government, provided for an initial period of tutelage during which the entire territory would be controlled by a governor, secretary, and three judges, all appointed by Congress. As soon as there were five thousand adult males in the territory, they would have the right to elect a general assembly, but the congressionally appointed governor would retain an absolute veto over the assembly's actions. Moreover, only an owner of fifty acres of land could vote, and no law should ever be passed affecting the obligation of private contracts. Provision was made for the formation of not less than three or more than five states in the area, each of which was to enter the union on equal terms with the existing states as soon as its population amounted to 60,000. Throughout the territory, both under the temporary government and after the formation of states, there must be freedom of religion, proportional representation in legislatures, trial by jury, habeas corpus, and the privileges of the common law. Slavery was permanently excluded.

These provisions embodied the principles which Congress and the Ohio Company thought necessary to make settlement attractive to land buyers. They also embodied the basic principles won in the Revolution, for the men who wrote them knew that unless these were guaranteed, few Americans, law-abiding or otherwise, would care to live in the region. Though the ordinance of 1787 was perhaps less liberal in some respects than that of 1784, it did offer the promise of self-government; it did offer greater security to property rights; and it did offer, by its prohibition of slavery, a more completely free society than could be found in most of the existing states.

The prohibition of slavery (which Jefferson had tried in vain to have incorporated in the earlier ordinance) was doubtless aimed at prospective buyers in New England, for New Englanders by this time had become strongly opposed to slavery. The members of the Ohio Company and the congressmen who worked with them may or may not have been opposed to it themselves, but in any case self-interest had once again aligned with principle to produce a beneficial result for the American people.

The two failed to combine so favorably in the treatment of the Southwest, the area west of the mountains and south of the Ohio River, which remained in the possession of Georgia, the Carolinas, and Virginia. But even here, in spite of the greedy squabbling of rival speculators, the period saw the foundations laid for creation and admission to the union of new, independent states. Throughout the war, in the face of the Indian menace, settlers poured into this rich territory, the ubiquitous speculator always with them or a little ahead of them. Cut off by the mountains from the governments to the eastward, the people were obliged to form governments for themselves if they wanted to have any at all.

The first settlers of North Carolina's western lands banded together in the Watauga Association as early as 1772 and exercised governmental functions until 1776, when the area was organized as Washington County. In 1782 the state began selling large quantities of this western land to eastern speculators, but other competing speculative interests were already at work in the region itself, and between the two the settlers were pulled and hauled in several directions at once. In 1784 the state legislature, under the influence of the eastern group of speculators, ceded sovereignty over Washington County to Congress, but the next year, influenced by the other group, repealed the act. The settlers themselves, taking the cession at face value, organized a new state, calling it Franklin, and demanded admission to the union. For the next three years there were two governments contesting the area, that of Franklin and that of North Carolina, not to mention the Spanish government, which was exerting its influence through bribery to pull the settlers into Spanish allegiance. North Carolina was able to reassert its control and do away with the state of Franklin, but only after actual fighting had occurred. The area was finally ceded permanently to the United States in 1790 and in 1796 became the state of Tennessee.

Meanwhile, the same kind of thing was going on immediately south of the Ohio in the region that Virginia had not turned over to Congress in 1784. Rival groups of speculators were busy here too, some working for separation, others for staying with Virginia. In 1786 the state passed an act enabling the westerners to become independent on condition they join the United States (not Spain!), but it was 1792 before this new state of Kentucky was actually created. Much farther north the squabbles of New York and New Hampshire over the land along the Connecticut River led the settlers to organize a government of their own as early as 1777. Here too land speculation complicated the dispute, which did not finally end until New York renounced her claims in 1790 and the state of Vermont was admitted to the union in 1791.

Though the story of Kentucky and Tennessee and Vermont was not a happy one, there is no evidence of an intent to keep the people of these regions in a dependent status. Taken as a whole, the record of the Confederation with regard to the West showed real progress, especially by comparison with the static years of British control. England acquired secure title to the West in the peace of 1763. She acquired it after considerable deliberation, as the result of a decision that this region had a greater future than the sugar islands of the West Indies, which she could have chosen instead. Yet between 1763 and 1774 she failed to provide any civil government for the area. In 1774 she provided one in the Quebec Act by extending the boundaries of Quebec, with its autocratic government and Roman Catholic church, to cover the entire territory north of the Ohio and west of the Alleghenies, a move that infuriated the Americans who wished to settle there. Congress, on the other hand, within little more than three years after it acquired the Northwest not only provided for sale and settlement of the lands but developed a complete program for westward expansion on republican principles, a program that with little alteration carried the United States to its present continental limits.

The record of "the critical period" on the economic front was checkered. The first years of peace posed an extraordinary problem for Americans. For a century and a half, in spite of the notoriety of certain kinds of smuggling, their economic life had been adjusted to membership in the British Empire. The Navigation Acts, as we have seen, caused no great hardships: the colonists were content for the most part to ship their raw materials to the mother country and take her manufactures in return. In 1776 when the old channels of trade were abruptly closed, American merchants turned to privateering and to trade with France. But when peace returned in 1783, American consumers were clamoring for the familiar old British goods.

For a time it looked as though American merchants would be able to supply them in the old manner. In England Adam Smith's *Wealth of Nations*, preaching the gospel of free trade, had been published in the same year as the Declaration of Independence, and the British government in 1783 included several high officials, particularly the Earl of Shelburne and William Pitt the younger, who had been converted to the new doctrine. Benjamin Franklin worked hard in the peace negotiations to win commercial reciprocity for the United States, and Pitt and Shelburne favored granting it, but in spite of their efforts England decided that the Americans should not eat their cake and have it too. They might purchase British manufactures if they chose, the more the better, and English merchants would buy their tobacco. But they could not send their ships to British ports in the West Indies. Without this outlet for their fish and farm produce the Americans found themselves unable to meet their bills, and a deep depression settled over the country.

In France Thomas Jefferson, serving as American ambassador, struggled to open up new markets for his countrymen, and throughout the rest of the world American merchants began to explore what other opportunities there might be. They sailed their ships into European, African, and Asian ports wherever the local government would allow them and often where it would not. But for a time the going was rough and the results sparse.

At home Americans began to reconsider some old assumptions. Before the Revolution most people had assumed that manufacturing could not be profitable for Americans because of the high cost of labor in a country so full of free land and so short on labor. But the Revolution had obliged Americans to make things for themselves that they had formerly imported. They had begun when the nonimportation agreements obliged them to, and the war that followed, with the British blockading their coasts, had made self-help a continuing necessity. When the war ended, the buying spree that ran them into debt and depression reminded them that manufacturing might still be a political and moral necessity, even if it did not appear to be economically profitable.

"The Critical Period"

The nonimportation agreements, which first directed Americans seriously toward manufactures, had in fact tapped a rich vein in the American character: the desire to bring pressure on England turned even before the war into an urge for self-sufficiency. Native American manufactures were extolled not simply as a means to an end but as a form of virtue. There was for the Protestant American, deeply committed to the virtue of thrift, something morally appealing in avoiding the importation of foreign goods and making do with what one could manufacture at home. If God demanded that an individual improve his talents, it was obvious that a nation too should husband its resources and not spend its money on things it could make for itself.

In order to further this end after the artificial stimulus of war had ceased, many states passed protective tariffs giving local manufactures an advantage over foreign imports (but usually exempting imports from other states in the Confederation). But the attempt to protect domestic manufactures in this way could not be effective unless all the states adopted identical regulations. Otherwise the importation of foreign manufactures into a state with no or low tariffs would overflow into all the other states. What was needed was a national regulation of trade, and that the Articles of Confederation did not sanction. Despite this deficiency, the economic history of these years was not entirely gloomy. Americans had known periods of depression as colonists too; with independence they were at least free to find their own way out. And by 1787, with new trade routes and new markets opening up, the depression had begun to lift.

The country gave signs of its social sanity by the speed with which the wounds of war were healed in the rehabilitation of colonists who had remained loyal to the King. If the American Revolution was in any sense a civil war, the Confederation did a much faster and much better job of reconstruction than the United States did after Appomattox. How many thousand loyalists departed for Canada or England is not known, but whatever their number their places were quickly filled. Of those who stayed behind, many suffered loss of property and, for a time, of political rights, but the end of the Confederation period saw them reabsorbed into the community on equal terms with no enduring heritage of bitterness.

The social health of the new nation was also apparent in the proliferation of intellectual activity following the war. National pride found expression in appeals for an American culture, and though the appeals were frequently more eloquent than the response, there was an astonishing production of historical writing, verse, painting, and even schoolbooks dedicated to magnifying America. New scientific societies were begun, notably the American Academy of Arts and Sciences at Boston, while the older American Philosophical Society breathed a new vigor. Companies of eager reformers sprang up everywhere and organized to improve agriculture, remodel penal codes, abolish slavery, prevent drunkenness, help immigrants, build libraries. The Americans were already embarked on their tireless, and to many Europeans tiresome, campaign to improve themselves and the world.

Although the perspective of nearly two centuries enables us to see the United States of the 1780's as a healthy, thriving young nation, there were many Americans at the time who thought otherwise. The achievements of the period just outlined, except in western policy, were the work either of the state governments or of smaller groups or of individuals. Only in relation to the West could the national government point to any notable accomplishment, and only in relation to the West did it really have any power to act independently of the state governments. True, it had supervised the war and the negotiation of the peace, but those who had participated in the government during that time were aware of how heavily they had leaned on France. Congress had found it much easier to get both troops and money from France than from the states, a fact which dimmed the pride they felt in victory.

As for the peace, reliance on France had led Congress to impose a shameful set of conditions on its diplomats, namely, that they follow French dictates in everything except insistence on independence. Only by ignoring their instructions had the United States ministers been able to secure the terms which gave Americans land west of the Appalachians. Even at that it was not the strength of the United States but rather the rivalry of England and France that had made possible the negotiation of such favorable terms. England had been generous in an attempt to drive a wedge between the United States and her ally.

After the war, American diplomats in Europe felt for the first time the full meaning of their country's impotence. Jefferson, who took Franklin's post in France, found the job an excellent school of humility, and John Adams at the Court of St. James's was treated with studied contempt, while England steadfastly refused to grant a commercial treaty and clung to her trading posts in the Northwest area in direct violation of the peace treaty. Spain, left in undisputed possession of the Mississippi for three hundred miles from its mouth, closed the port of New Orleans to American commerce in the not unreasonable hope of detaching Kentucky and Tennessee. The American frontiersmen there could scarcely exist unless they could float their produce to market via the Mississippi, and yet Congress almost agreed to a proposed treaty negotiated by John Jay, that would have yielded for twenty-five or thirty years whatever claim the United States had to navigation of the river through Spanish territory. In return eastern merchants would have obtained commercial privileges in Spain. Since the American claim was a very dubious one at best, the treaty was not a bad one, and it received a majority of votes in Congress, though not the necessary nine-state majority. It nevertheless antagonized the westerners, whose interests it seemed to sacrifice to those of eastern merchants.

In retrospect it is possible to see that the diplomatic failures of the Confederation period were the result of forces that lay beyond the control of the United States in its infant condition. Though independent, its three million people scarcely constituted a world power. No matter how their national government had been constructed, they could not have carried a big enough stick to command respect in Europe. But this thought, when it occurred to people at the time, was cold comfort. Men like Washington, Madison, Hamilton, Jay, John Adams, Robert Morris, men who had caught a vision of American greatness, wished to see it translated into fact without delay. As they struggled to operate the government they had created and repeatedly found themselves blocked by a lack of power, they became increasingly convinced that greatness would never attend a country whose government rested so helplessly on the capricious sufferance of thirteen superior state governments.

These men did what they could to make the national government under the Articles of Confederation as strong as that document and the prevailing temper of the state delegations would allow. Even before the Articles were formally put into operation, they moved to consolidate administrative responsibility by appointment of separate secretaries to manage each of the important activities with which the government must be concerned: foreign affairs, war, and finance. Hitherto the United States had no real executive departments, the matters requiring continuous attention being handled by various congressional committees. In January, 1781, a Department of Foreign Affairs was created and in February the departments of Finance and War, each to be run by one man who would be responsible to Congress and hold office during its pleasure.

"The Critical Period"

In selecting a Superintendent of Finance, Congress was fortunate in having available Robert Morris, a leading Philadelphia merchant. Morris was able to bring a semblance of order into the chaos he encountered upon undertaking the job. Though he had to beg and borrow from state governments and from foreign countries, and though he seems to have mingled private gain too closely with public, he kept the United States almost solvent during the remainder of the war. In order to assist him, Congress authorized the first national bank on May 26, 1781, thus exercising a power that was to be a matter of controversy for some time to come.

In appointing heads of the other departments, Congress made less fortunate choices. Robert R. Livingston, the first Secretary for Foreign Affairs, was elected with the active assistance of the French minister La Luzerne in August, 1781, but resigned the following year and was not replaced by John Jay until 1784. Jay, like Livingston, was more ready to listen to the demands of other countries than was proper in a secretary whose business was to bargain with them. The office of Secretary at War was held successively by Benjamin Lincoln and Henry Knox, neither of them distinguished. Nevertheless, the very existence of secretaries whose sole business was to administer a department and who could be held responsible for its activities was a considerable advance in the creation of an effective national government. Each department developed a small staff of workers who became the first professional civil servants of the United States and in many cases continued to work in the same capacities under the new government after the Confederation ended.

But the creation of administrative departments did not in itself furnish the power to take necessary or desirable actions. After the Articles of Confederation were adopted, the more nationalistic congressmen began to feel out the possibilities of a more effective central government by suggesting that Congress had by implication the power to use whatever means were necessary to carry out its functions. As long as the war with England lasted, they frequently persuaded the other members to take bold actions, as in creating the national bank, laying an embargo on trade with England, or giving Washington authority to impress food and supplies. But the members were not yet ready to ask, nor would the states have been willing to grant, a general authority to execute laws. Once the war ceased and united action became less urgent, Congress became increasingly timid about asserting itself, and its strength ebbed rapidly. There was even a reversion in administration: Robert Morris resigned as Superintendent of Finance and a committee took charge again.

As Congress spoke in feebler tones, the state governments grew contemptuous of its authority. They violated the Articles of Confederation by ignoring the nation's treaties with foreign countries, by waging war with the Indians, by building navies of their own. They sent men with less vision and less ability to represent them and at times failed to send any, so that Congress could scarcely muster a quorum to do business. They refused to fill congressional requisitions any better than they had those imposed by Great Britain during their colonial days.

As in the years before Confederation, it was in financial matters that the impotence of the national government was most acutely felt. From 1780 when its paper money became worthless until 1787 when it began to realize a small income from the sale of public lands, the government was totally dependent, except for loans, on the unobliging states. Congress sought a remedy by proposing an amendment to the Articles of Confederation giving the United States the right to levy and collect a 5 per cent duty on foreign imports. Amendment, however, required unanimous acceptance and in 1782 failed because Rhode Island, the smallest state of the union, flatly rejected it, while the other states attached various conditions to their acceptance. In the following year Congress tried again by coupling the proposal with a number of others designed to win favor for it. By 1786 every state but New York was ready to agree in some form, but New York's refusal was enough to defeat the scheme once more.

It had become clear, to the country's leaders at least, that Congress as then constituted could never perform its functions. When the Articles of Confederation were drafted, Americans had had little experience of what a national government could do for them and bitter experience of what an arbitrary government could do to them. In creating a central government they were therefore more concerned with keeping it under control than with giving it the means to do its job. Their state governments, they felt, should hold a leading rein on this new power. State governments were closer to home, closer to the people, and could be relied on to prevent Congress from getting the bit in its teeth and rushing into tyranny.

Time had by no means disappointed these calculations: Congress had never got out of hand. But anyone with half an eye for the nation's welfare could see by 1787 that the state governments had proved unworthy masters. They would not allow Congress to act whether action was needed or not. Congress had been safeguarded into impotency, its deliberations rendered as ineffective as those of a debating society, while the states grew ever stronger. Washington had seen what was happening and warned against it as early as 1780: "I see one head gradually changing into thirteen. . . . I see the powers of Congress declining too fast for the consequence and respect which is due to them as the grand representative body of America." In the summer of 1787 James Wilson sadly confirmed the fact:

"The Critical Period"

Among the first sentiments expressed in the first Congress one was that Virginia is no more, that Massachusetts is no more, that Pennsylvania is no more. We are now one nation of brethren. We must bury all local interests and distinctions. This language continued for some time. The tables at length began to turn. No sooner were the State Governments formed than their jealousy and ambition began to display themselves. Each endeavored to cut a slice from the common loaf, to add to its own morsel, till at length the confederation became frittered down to the impotent condition in which it now stands.

As the state governments grew stronger, they grew, in the opinion of many of their leading citizens, more irresponsible not only toward the nation but toward their own people. The Revolution had begun because the British government violated the sacredness of private property. Now it seemed that some of the state governments were doing the same by failing to protect the investments of creditors. Rhode Island, where a wildly depreciating paper currency had been made legal tender, was the notorious example. Hordes of happy debtors there were paying off their obligations in worthless paper, leaving their creditors bankrupt. Or so the newspapers said, and from past experience everyone was ready to believe the worst of Rhode Island.

And so, in addition to the need for a government which could act effectively for the nation, there began to be felt the need for a central authority with power to meet this new threat to property rights. Without such an authority, it was feared by many, the whole country would degenerate into anarchy. Was not property the only real security for life and liberty? Those who felt this way saw a dreadful portent for the future in what had happened in Massachusetts in the autumn of 1786. Farmers in the western part of the state, hit hard by a combination of low prices and high taxes, rose in armed rebellion under Daniel Shays. Shays and his men closed the courts in Berkshire, Hampshire, and Worcester counties, thus

"The Critical Period"

ending suits at law and preventing creditors from collecting debts. They defied the state government; and if the loyal militia of the state had not come to the rescue, the United States arsenal at Springfield would have fallen to an armed mob, with the central government helpless to prevent it. Without men or money it would be equally helpless to cope with future, possibly worse, threats of anarchy.

The prospects of remedying the situation looked dim, for with the states so powerful and so irresponsible it was unlikely they would agree to give up their death grip on the central government. Even if the majority of them should be willing, one dissent was sufficient to prevent amendment of the Articles of Confederation. But while wise men shook their heads over Daniel Shays and talked hysterically of the advantages of monarchy or dictatorship, events were already stirring which would give the United States a government true to the principles of the Revolution and commensurate with the national vision of its greatest leaders.

X

The Constitutional Convention

The year 1786 was the low point of the Critical Period. It was the year of Shays' Rebellion, the year of John Jay's proposed treaty with Spain, a year in which the depression in trade reached its lowest ebb. In the midst of discouragements Virginia took the lead in an attempt to breathe a little life into the national government. She proposed an interstate convention to discuss a uniform regulation of commerce. If the delegates could agree on a set of recommendations, the states might then authorize Congress to carry them out. Several states expressed a readiness to take up Virginia's proposal, and the meeting was scheduled for Annapolis, Maryland, on the first Monday in September, 1786.

Not much is known about the maneuvering that preceded the Annapolis convention, but there is evidence that some of the commissioners saw in it the opportunity to inaugurate a thorough overhaul of the Articles of Confederation. New Jersey sent a delegation empowered to consider not only commerce but "other important matters." New York sent Alexander Hamilton, an ardent nationalist, and Virginia sent James Madison, who wrote to Jefferson a month earlier that "Gentlemen both within and without Congress wish to make this meeting subservient to a

The Constitutional Convention

plenipotentiary convention for amending the Confederation." At the time he wrote, Madison doubted the possibility of effecting so happy an object, but when the commissioners from five states, New York, New Jersey, Pennsylvania, Delaware, and Virginia, assembled at Annapolis in September, they found themselves agreed on the need for more extended reforms than most of them were empowered to suggest. Though delegates from other states were still on the way to the meeting, those present hastily adopted a report (said to have been drafted by Hamilton) calling for a general convention at Philadelphia in May, 1787. This convention, it was hoped, would make recommendations "to render the constitution of the Federal Government adequate to the exigencies of the Union." Without waiting for latecomers the commissioners sent their report to all the states and to Congress and then headed home.

Several states, led again by Virginia, responded directly to this invitation by appointing delegates, and the caliber of the Virginia delegation, headed by Washington himself, disclosed the importance which that state, at least, attached to the meeting. Other states, regarding the proposal as revolutionary—which it was— refused to take action until Congress passed a resolution urging attendance as "the most probable means of establishing in these states a firm national government."

Under these auspices twenty-nine of the most distinguished men in the United States made their appearance in the Philadelphia State House on May 25, 1787. In the course of the meetings twenty-six more took their seats. Rhode Island alone failed to participate. Washington, who was chosen president of the convention on its first day, lent it a dignity everyone was bound to respect, a dignity further enhanced by the venerable presence of Benjamin Franklin. The other members were mostly younger men in their thirties and forties, old enough to have lived and fought and thought through the crowded years of the Revolution, old enough to have digested the significance of those years, not old enough to think them all vanity and vexation of spirit.

There were a few conspicuous absences. Sam Adams of Massachusetts and Patrick Henry of Virginia were not there, the latter because he "smelled a rat" in the whole proceeding. Both had become politically myopic in their old age and were well left at home. Thomas Jefferson and John Adams, who might have contributed much, were in Europe, but Jefferson's views were ably represented by James Madison, and Adams' by Gouverneur Morris of Pennsylvania, a dazzling speaker and thinker of conservative tastes.

Much has been written about these men and their work, and since we are still intimately affected by what they did, we cannot view them with complete detachment. Indeed, as long as patriotism remained the principal ingredient of American historical writing, the constitutional convention was regarded as an assemblage of the gods. But in 1913 Charles Beard published *An Economic Interpretation of the Constitution of the United States,* and, ever since, historians have striven to look at the convention as a meeting of ordinary human beings. Beard's achievement was extraordinary: he examined the career of every member of the convention and discovered that most of them had invested in public securities of the United States and therefore stood to gain by strengthening public credit. He also examined their political ideas as expressed in the convention and found that most of them wished to restrain the people from legislation that would adversely affect the value of public securities. The conclusion was obvious that the makers of the Constitution, consciously or unconsciously, were seeking to protect their own economic interests, a characteristic that historians of the present age have frequently discovered in the actions of men both past and present.

We have discovered signs of economic interest in the events of the decades preceding the convention. The colonists did not wish to see their trade ruined or their property endangered by Parliamentary taxation and fought to protect themselves; land speculators wished to profit by settling the West and helped to secure a national domain. In each case self-interest led to the enunciation of principles which went far beyond the point at issue. In each case the people of the United States were committed to doctrines which helped to mold their future in ways they could not have anticipated. At the constitutional convention much the same thing occurred. The members had a selfish interest in bringing about a public good. But in this case, contrary to the impression given by Beard, it is all but impossible to differentiate private selfishness from public spirit.

Patriotism led responsible Americans to invest in public securities in wartime, and patriotism guided their efforts to revive the languishing nation which their money and blood had purchased. That personal economic interests were also involved is undeniable, but we learn very little about the convention by knowing that its members held public securities and believed in the sacredness of property. The principles they carried with them to Philadelphia would not all have fitted in their pocketbooks. How little they can be explained by economic or class interests alone may be suggested by a look at the views of one blunt-spoken member from Connecticut.

Beard found Roger Sherman's political philosophy adequately expressed in his statement that the national legislature ought to be elected by the state legislatures rather than by direct vote, that the people "immediately shoud have as little to do as may be about the government. They want information and are constantly liable to be misled." Taken by itself this statement seems to warrant Beard's conclusion that Sherman "believed in reducing the popular influence in the new government to the minimum." But look at what Sherman said at other times and about other parts of the new government. On June 4, four days after he made the statement above, he spoke against giving the President a veto power over laws, because he "was against enabling any one man to stop the will of the whole. No one man could be found so far above all the rest in wisdom." On June 21 he argued for election of the House of Representatives by the state legislatures, but after election by the people had been decided upon, spoke for annual elections as against triennial, because he "thought the Representatives ought to return home and mix with the people." Throughout the convention he sought to preserve for the small states the same disproportionate share of power they enjoyed under the Articles of Confederation, but on July 14 he opposed those who wished to retain a predominance in the national government of the existing states against any new ones, insisting that the people of new states in the West would be "our posterity" and ought not to be discriminated against. Three days later he was against election of the President by the people, but on August 14 he was in favor of substantial pay for congressmen, because otherwise "men ever so fit could not serve unless they were at the same time rich."

Whatever explanation may be offered for these views, they represent a much broader conception of society and government and a much greater confidence in the people than might be inferred from the single remark by which Beard characterized the man. And Sherman was no exceptional figure. There was scarcely a member of the convention whose views can be explained by any simple formula, economic or otherwise. Even Alexander Hamilton, who deserted the convention for a time when it would not establish an executive and a senate with life terms, argued for a larger house of representatives than the convention would agree to: "He was seriously of opinion that the House of Representatives was on so narrow a scale as to be really dangerous, and to warrant a jealousy in the people for their liberties." Pierce Butler of South Carolina, who held public securities himself and argued vociferously that representation in the legislature should be apportioned among the different states according to wealth (the only part of his political philosophy Beard thought worth mentioning) was against placing any property qualification on the suffrage, saying, "There is no right of which the people are more jealous than that of suffrage." Holland, he observed, where the right had been abridged, had turned into a "rank aristocracy." As for those who speculated in public securities, he was against requiring the new government to pay the public debt in full "lest it should compel payment as well to the Blood-suckers who had speculated on the distresses of others, as to those who had fought and bled for their country."

The members of the convention were certainly human, which is to say they were complex, unpredictable, paradoxical, compounded of rationality and irrationality, moved by selfishness and by altruism, by love and by hate and by anger—and by principle. If the convention succeeded, it was not simply because the members possessed a common economic or class interest but because they held common principles, principles learned in twenty years of British tyranny and American seeking, in colonial assemblies, in state legislatures, and in Congress. Their work has often been described as a bundle of compromises, and so it was, but the compromises were almost all on matters of detail. They could afford to give and take where they disagreed, because there were so many important things about which they did agree.

The Constitutional Convention

They agreed, to begin with, on the urgency of their task. Most of them were convinced that unless they came up with an acceptable, and at the same time workable, scheme of national government, the union would dissolve. Charles Pinckney of South Carolina, who had just been serving in Congress, believed that body would have collapsed already if the appointment of the convention had not given hope that the union might continue. But he did not need to tell the other members. Whenever arguments became heated, they would remind each other of the dreadful consequences if they failed. "The condition of the United States requires that something should be immediately done," cried Gunning Bedford of Delaware, himself a strong advocate of states' rights. "The fate of the Union will be decided by the Convention," said Elbridge Gerry of Massachusetts. "It is agreed on all hands," said his colleague Caleb Strong, "that Congress are nearly at an end. If no Accommodation takes place, the Union itself must soon be dissolved."

No one liked to think what would happen if the union did dissolve. Great Britain was still clinging to her posts in the Northwest in anticipation of the event. Spain was tugging insistently at the Southwest. If the union fell, each would move in for the kill. John Dickinson, one of the members from Delaware, who had been present at the Stamp Act Congress in 1765, must have recalled grimly the fears he felt then. In a memorable letter to William Pitt he had pleaded that the colonies not be driven to fight: they would win, he had been sure of that; but the fruit of their victory would be "A multitude of Commonwealths, Crimes and Calamities, Centuries of mutual Jealousies, Hatreds, Wars of Devastation; till at last the exhausted Provinces shall sink into Slavery under the yoke of some fortunate Conqueror." Now the crimes and calamities had begun—what else was Shays' rebellion? And unless the convention could resuscitate the national government, the rest of the prophecy would horribly follow.

The Constitutional Convention

Dickinson and the other members agreed not only on the desperateness of the situation but, in broad outlines at least, on what must be done about it. They almost all believed that the central government should be strengthened by enabling it to act without the mediation of state governments, to levy and collect its own taxes, and to make laws and enforce them through its own administrative agencies. There were a few members, notably from the smaller states, who felt that the task of the convention could be fulfilled simply by granting more authority to the existing government, in other words to Congress. But this solution was generally regarded as dangerous. Congress was not, strictly speaking, a representative body: its members were not elected directly by the people. To give it powers of taxation and legislation would therefore be to violate a cardinal principle of the Revolution. Moreover, even if popularly elected, Congress might by means of these powers get out of control. While it operated through the state governments, they served as a restraint on it, far too great a one. Before it could be safely freed from that restraint and given the strength everyone agreed it should have, it must be made truly representative and must be furnished with some new safeguard against abuse of its authority.

The new safeguard that most of the delegates at Philadelphia had in mind was a division of the central government into several different departments, each independent of the others, each with carefully specified powers. The appeal of this method was obvious: it had undergone testing for ten years in the state governments; therefore Americans could with some confidence judge its success and measure its failure.

The state constitutions, as we have seen, were constructed with this very intention of keeping the different departments separate and independent, but it was now felt that this intention had not been carried out with complete success. The state legislatures,

except in Pennsylvania, were bicameral, but the upper houses were not much wiser or more virtuous or more conservative than the lower houses and did not constitute a sufficient check. And while the legislatures had been protected from the governors, the governors had not been protected from the legislatures. John Adams' warning that the executive must be given strength had gone unheeded. The legislatures had run away with the governments, and the lower houses had run away with the legislatures.

These failures to keep the different departments adequately separated did not reduce the general confidence in the principle of separation itself. They were failures of application, from which the convention could learn what to avoid in forming the national government. Under the Articles of Confederation there had been the even more serious failure of not applying the principle at all. All the functions and powers of government had been concentrated in a single body of men, a mistake that might have resulted in tyranny if Congress had not been kept so weak by the jealousy of the states. As Edmund Randolph of Virginia put it, "If the union of these powers heretofore in Congress has been safe, it has been owing to the general impotency of that body." The problem then was to construct a representative government of divided powers on the model of the state governments but without the flaws which ten years' wear and tear had brought to light.

There was no serious consideration of any radically different design: a few members, notably Alexander Hamilton and John Dickinson, thought highly of constitutional monarchy as a form of government, but they knew that Americans could not be sold that idea. And the other members, the great majority, wanted nothing but a republic: they were committed irrevocably to the principle of equality as expressed in the Declaration of Independence, and that principle, they believed, demanded republican government. Some

The Constitutional Convention

of them had doubts about the durability of a large republic but were willing to leave the proof to time. Even Elbridge Gerry, who said that "the evils we experience flow from the excess of democracy," and that democracy was "the worst ... of all political evils," nevertheless believed that the United States should remain a republic.

With so large an area of agreement it was easy for the delegates to determine the main outlines of the government they wished to establish. On the third day of their meetings Edmund Randolph presented a series of resolutions, drafted by his colleague James Madison, which after three and a half months of discussion, amendment, and expansion emerged as the United States Constitution. Randolph's resolutions provided for a national executive, a national judiciary, and a bicameral national legislature, the lower house to be popularly elected and representation in both houses to be proportioned either to population or to amount of taxation. With one qualification, which we shall examine, these provisions were accepted. Although William Paterson of New Jersey presented a rival plan, in which the national government was to remain under the undivided control of Congress, it was overwhelmingly rejected. There was never any serious dispute about the main features of the Randolph plan.

It was in the details that particular interests of a selfish or local nature sought expression and at times threatened to wreck the convention. That it was not wrecked was owing in part to the fact that nearly every member was willing to give way to majority opinion in order to insure success and in part to the fact that a majority opinion could be formed on the crucial questions by appealing to the fundamental principle of equality. The members differed widely in their views as to how the principle should operate, but none could deny its supremacy.

The Constitutional Convention

The most serious disagreement over its application came between the delegates from the large states and those from the small. In the existing Confederation the principle had been applied to give every state an equal weight in the government. By the rejection of Paterson's plan and the acceptance of Randolph's it was determined that this should not be the case in the new constitution, but the small states still fought for as large a role as they could get in the new government. They argued, for example, that the state governments should choose all officers of the national government, and they demanded equal representation for states in the upper house of the legislature if not in the lower.

The delegates from the large states were against this kind of equality and argued instead for the equality of men rather than states. It is obvious that this position suited their interests: if all men were represented equally in the government, the large states would have more representatives than the small. But the principle of equality, as we have seen, has generally been advanced in conjunction with someone's interest, and it can scarcely be denied that the application advocated by the large states was the broader of the two. Though the Declaration of Independence had affirmed the equality of states in claiming for Americans a separate and equal station with other peoples of the earth, it had presented the principle itself in broader terms. It had said that all men, not all states, are created equal. And the delegates from the large states rang the changes on this theme throughout the convention. "Can we forget for whom we are forming a Government?" asked James Wilson. "Is it for *men,* or for the imaginary beings called *States?*" And his opponents could give no real answer.

Unfortunately the delegates of the large states did not all extend the principle beyond the Appalachian Mountains. Though they believed all easterners equal, some of them thought that the

The Constitutional Convention

government should be so constructed as to prevent the future states that were forming west of the mountains from ever dominating it. Gouverneur Morris, who spoke passionately against "state attachments" and urged the delegates from the small states "to extend their views beyond the present moment of time; beyond the narrow limits of place," was the next moment himself arguing that "the rule of representation ought to be so fixed as to secure to the Atlantic States a prevalence in the National Councils."

The small states, on the other hand, welcomed the idea of new and equal states in the West which would reduce the predominance of the large eastern states. They opposed Gouverneur Morris' attempt to keep western representation inferior and supported a proposal (which it is only fair to say was also advocated by many of the most able large-state delegates) that a census of the country be taken at regular intervals and made the basis of representation in the lower house (one representative for every 40,000 persons). In this way new states would be assured representation on the same scale as the old.

Through their support of this measure, which was successful, the small states helped to further the equality of men, but at the same time they wrung from the large states a concession that still impairs the functioning of that principle. By threatening to bolt the convention they won equal representation for states in the Senate. These two provisions, equality for states in the Senate and for men in the House of Representatives (to be regularly reapportioned as population grew), were the principal features of the so-called "great compromise." It was actually more of a concession than a compromise, for the large states got nothing from it, but it did successfully break the convention's worst impasse.

That impasse had taken the form of a dispute between large and small states, but a more ominous conflict had lain beneath it, a

139

conflict between North and South. In the Continental Congress representatives from the two sections had become more and more suspicious of each other, and the voting had become increasingly polarized. Each section feared that its interests might suffer in a government in which the other held a dominant position. Although the northern states had a majority of the free population, it was expected that the preponderance would shift to the South (the Southwest was already filling up much more rapidly than the Northwest). The compromise thus offered something to both sections: by providing for equal representation of states in the Senate, it gave to the South a present assurance against a northern majority and to the North a future assurance against an expected southern majority.

What divided the two sections most sharply was slavery and the fear of the South that a northern majority would destroy the institution. No one in the convention had a good word to say for slavery. No one could blink the fact that it violated directly, openly, and deliberately the principle of equality that had animated the Revolution and that was now directing the creation of a national government. But if no one would speak in favor of slavery, neither could anyone insist on abolition. To have done so would have been to end the convention. The very power that the idea of equality had already demonstrated made southerners more fearful that their huge investment in slave labor would fall before it. When the principle of equality encountered the South's vested interest in slavery, the conflict was irreconcilable, and in the summer of 1787 it was equality that had to give ground. While the great compromise upheld equality by making population the sole basis of apportioning representation in the lower house, it also belied the principle by a provision that gave southerners an extra share in the government. The provision for apportioning representation (and direct taxation) dictated that, in counting population, three-fifths of the slaves in any state should be included. The free population of the state thereby received a bonus in political power because of their slaves.

Even after the great compromise, the subject continued to trouble the convention. Several northern members aggressively denounced slavery and the slave trade, and Roger Sherman spoke what was probably the sentiment of most northerners when he said that if the national government were given the authority to prohibit the slave trade, it would be morally incumbent upon it to exercise that authority. Sherman also said, however, and again spoke for the majority, that if the southern states insisted on the right to import slaves, this was not too high a price to pay for their membership in the union. An agreement was finally reached whereby the government was not to prohibit the trade before the year 1808 but might impose a tax of not more than ten dollars per slave imported. It was also agreed that fugitive slaves escaping to a free state should be returned to their owners.

The majority of the convention knew that in these measures they had thrown equality to the winds. But the sacrifice purchased the continuation of the union and made possible a national government. At the moment, those objectives seemed to be worth the price.

The power left to the state governments was more than the most ardent nationalists would have liked, for the central government was not given the authority they would have assigned it to veto state laws. Moreover, while the House of Representatives was to be popularly elected, the manner of choosing both senators and presidential electors was left to the state legislatures. On the other hand, the Constitution and the laws and treaties made under it were to be the supreme law of the land, enforceable in both state and national courts. And the states were expressly forbidden to enact certain obnoxious types of legislation, such as bills of attainder, customs duties, paper-money laws, and laws impairing the obligation of contracts.

These prohibitions, it was hoped, would restore the security of property in states where the legislatures had proved unworthy guardians of it. The national government itself was protected from a runaway legislature by an executive with real veto power and a supreme judiciary with tenure during good behavior. The judges, it was understood, would necessarily pass on the constitutionality of congressional legislation whenever suits were brought to it.

In spite of the concessions to state power, the members of the convention knew that there would be objections from the state governments to a national constitution which so sharply reduced their authority. In order to bypass them and to rest the government where genuine constitutional government must rest, on the people, the convention provided that the Constitution, after transmission to Congress and from Congress to the states, should be approved or rejected by specially elected conventions in every state. In order to prevent two or three or even four states from frustrating the union of the rest, ratification by nine states was to put the Constitution in operation among those nine.

It was not a document that gave entire satisfaction to anyone. Edmund Randolph, who had introduced the resolutions on which it was based, could not bring himself to sign it. But most of the members thought it was as good as could be expected and infinitely preferable to the existing government, if the expiring Congress could be called a government.

While those who felt this way were fixing their signatures to the document, Benjamin Franklin was looking at the gilded sun carved on the presiding officer's high-backed chair. Turning to the members near him, he said, with his usual felicity, that painters had "found it difficult to distinguish in their art a rising from a setting sun. I have ... often and often in the course of the Session, and the vicissitudes of my hopes and fears as to its issue, looked at that behind the President without being able to tell whether it was rising or setting: But now at length I have the happiness to know that it is a rising and not a setting Sun."

XI

Ratification

Franklin of course was right, but neither he nor any of those to whom he spoke could have been sure he was right at the time. The members of the convention were much more aware of the national danger, much more eager to see their efforts succeed, than were the rest of the population. They knew, as their constituents could not, that each provision of the new Constitution was the outcome of extended discussion, of mutual forbearance, concession, compromise, the result of a combined desire to protect the nation without excessive injury to local interests.

As the Constitution went out to the states, people scanning its provisions in the columns of their local newspapers seldom realized that a provison they did not like might be a *sine qua non* to the other fellow four hundred or six hundred miles away. Nor did people generally feel that the national government required such drastic revision in order to preserve the union. Oh, they all knew that Congress was too feeble, needed bucking up, but this new Constitution was no mere starch to stiffen the Articles of Confederation. This was a whole new government, and so far as they could see, it was much more powerful than their state governments and (what was worse) much farther beyond their control.

Ratification

They admitted that the central government needed an independent income. They had agreed in every state but one to give it a
5 per cent duty on imports, but what did this new Constitution say?
"The Congress shall have power to lay and collect taxes, duties,
imposts, and excises." With such unlimited power, Congress could
squeeze the people dry. There would be nothing left for the state
governments, which would quickly die in the contest with this
superior authority.

The prospect was not calculated to please local politicians, and as
the convention had anticipated, they were among the loudest
objectors to the new plan. Again and again they warned that its
adoption would be the death knell not only of the state governments but of the popular liberties which the constitutions of those
governments protected. Nearly every state constitution contained a
bill of rights protecting trial by jury, freedom of speech, freedom of
assembly, freedom of religion, freedom from quartering of troops,
freedom from search except by warrant, and the other processes of
common law. These guarantees were missing from the federal
Constitution; and though its advocates pointed out that the United
States government would be empowered to do only those things
which the Constitution authorized it to do, the opposition rightly
answered that without a bill of rights to limit it the government
might constitutionally employ tyrannical means to carry out its
authorized functions.

But what seems to have worried the opponents of the Constitution most was the scale of representation. The assemblies of the
different states varied considerably in size, but in none was the ratio
of representatives to population nearly as small as that established
by the Constitution. The first federal House of Representatives
would contain only fifty-five members, a much smaller number to
make laws for the whole nation than was required in most states to

make state laws. After a census had been taken, the representation was not to "exceed one for every thirty thousand" (the figure had been reduced from forty thousand at the prompting of Washington), which could not raise the number much and might lower it; as the provision was phrased, it would be perfectly constitutional for Congress to set the ratio at one to one hundred thousand or one to two hundred thousand.

We can scarcely appreciate the alarm that this provision caused without recalling the prejudice existing at the time against the possibility of reconciling republican government with a large extent of territory. Through reading or misreading Montesquieu—no author was more widely cited in debates on the Constitution— many Americans were convinced that an effective national government for the United States must sooner or later depart from republican principles. James Madison had pointed out to the convention that this fear was groundless. In a republic, he argued both in the convention and afterward in the newspapers, the majority, however composed, will always rule. The danger to individual rights will come therefore from a majority. In a small republic the number of different groups and interests will be small enough and the opportunities of communication between them so easy that majorities will easily be formed and will tyrannize over the minority. But in a large republic the number of interests will be correspondingly larger and the opportunities for communication fewer. Consequently, the likelihood of a majority being formed against the interests of a minority is less.

Madison was right, and his argument, classically stated in the tenth number of *The Federalist,* a series of essays which he wrote with Alexander Hamilton and John Jay to support the Constitution, is perhaps the keenest analysis of political behavior ever written by an American. But Madison in 1788 was less heeded than Montesquieu. As they looked at the plan for the national House of Representatives, people saw in it the proof of Montesquieu's observations. How could six men, the number assigned to New York, represent the multifold interests of the people of that state? The function of a representative, Madison told them, was to sift the views of the multitude, to filter them through the medium of his own superior wisdom. That was why representative government was superior to pure democracy. But this was not the accepted notion of a representative. The job of a representative, as most Americans saw it, was that of an errand boy; he was to carry the views of his constituents to the legislature, and never mind about filtering them.

How then could fifty-five errand boys present the view of three million people? The answer was obvious: they could not and would not. Instead, they would represent the views of the most powerful and wealthy sections of the three million. Melancton Smith of Dutchess County, New York, one of the ablest opponents of the Constitution, showed that not only the upper house of the legislature but also the lower house would be monopolized by the wealthy and well-born. With the number of representatives so small and the election districts necessarily so large, the offices would carry much honor and be sought after by the kind of men whose birth and wealth would enable them to succeed.

Though they were less articulate in analyzing the danger, many ordinary voters feared that the few men who would represent them in a Congress hundreds of miles away would be bigger men, richer men, less familiar with their needs, less sensitive to their misfortunes than the common folk from their own towns or counties whom they sent to the state legislatures. Thus Amos Singletary, an old

Ratification

Massachusetts farmer who had served in the General Court back in 1775, lashed out helplessly at those who were trying to persuade him that the new government would not endanger his liberties.

agrarians

These lawyers, and men of learning, and moneyed men, that talk so finely, and gloss over matters so smoothly, to make us poor illiterate people swallow down the pill, expect to get into Congress themselves; they expect to be the managers of this Constitution, and get all the power and all the money into their own hands, and then they will swallow up all us little folks.

Not all "little folks" felt such dread of the new government. In the Massachusetts ratifying convention, where the protest just quoted was made, it was answered by another farmer who said he had learned the worth of good government by the want of it. He was referring to the disorders of Shays' Rebellion, which most Massachusetts farmers had disliked as much as the rest of the population had.

prob w/ Articles are to threatnig

Now, Mr. President, when I saw this Constitution, I found that it was a cure for these disorders. It was just such a thing as we wanted. I got a copy of it, and read it over and over. I had been a member of the Convention to form our own state constitution, and had learnt something of the checks and balances of power, and I found them all here. I did not go to any lawyer, to ask his opinion; we have no lawyer in our town, and we do well enough without. I formed my own opinion, and was pleased with this Constitution. My honorable old daddy there [pointing to Singletary] won't think that I expect to be a Congress-man and swallow up the liberties of the people.

The Constitution won acceptance partly because there were plain men like this who saw its virtues but also because men who were not so plain bent every effort to get it ratified. They not only talked finely and glossed over smoothly, but they used every political trick in the book. Where they thought reason and patience were called for, they used them; but where they thought vilification, slander, invective, and downright deception would help, they were not squeamish about using them either. How far they were willing to go became evident as soon as the Constitution was dispatched from the convention to Congress, then sitting at New York.

The procedure that had been prescribed was for Congress to receive the document first and transmit it to the state legislatures, which should then name times and places for their respective ratifying conventions. When nine of these had approved, the new government would be organized. But Congress reacted to the Constitution with less than unanimous enthusiasm and did not send it on to the states for ten days. This was too long for Pennsylvania, or at least for the "Federalists" there, as the advocates of the Constitution called themselves.

The Pennsylvania legislature had been holding its session in the upstairs chamber of the Philadelphia State House while downstairs the convention was putting the finishing touches on its work. On the morning of September 18, 1787, the day after the convention adjourned and sent the Constitution to Congress, the state assembly obtained an unofficial copy of it. On the following day it appeared in the newspapers, and before the week was out, the assault upon it had begun.

The assembly was to dissolve on September 29, and when by September 28 no official word had arrived from Congress, it looked as though the members would have to depart without summoning a ratifying convention. At this point the Federalists, alarmed by the rising tide of opposition, decided to act and had George Clymer, who until September 17 had been serving in the meeting downstairs, present a motion calling for a ratifying convention on November 30. There was a large enough majority to carry the motion, but before it could come to a vote, the noon recess interrupted the debate and allowed nineteen anti-Federalists (mostly westerners) to make their escape. They needed only to stay away to prevent any further business; for without them there would be no quorum, and the next day would end the session.

But on the next day the long awaited news from New York at last arrived, and the Federalists, feeling a little more righteous now, sent the sergeant at arms to round up the missing members. Only two were necessary to complete a quorum, and the sergeant found them at their lodgings. When they refused to accompany him, a mob was gathered—there were enough friends of the Constitution in Philadelphia to make a mob. While the two westerners trembled in helpless rage, the people carried them gleefully to the state house, deposited them in their seats, and barred the door against another escape. The necessary motions were then hilariously passed, with the date of the convention advanced to November 20.

During the few weeks until the Pennslyvania ratifying convention met, the two sides pummeled each other in the newspapers. About the debates in the convention we know very little, and for a good reason: the Federalists bought up the newspapers and printed only the speeches of their own party. Though a substantial Federalist majority had been elected to the convention, they apparently feared that popular pressure might reduce it if the arguments of the opposition should happen to appeal to the unpredictable populace. By December 15 they had pushed through a vote of acceptance. In Pennsylvania the Federalists plainly considered that the end justified the means.

Meanwhile Delaware, perceiving that the Constitution gave the small states as much as they could hope for, had already ratified, and New Jersey followed quickly without a dissenting voice. By the end of December one-third of the necessary adoptions had thus been secured, and in January, 1788, two more small states, Georgia and Connecticut, came in. It would not do, however, to construct the new government without the concurrence of the two remaining large states, Virginia and Massachusetts, or without New York, which was not so large in population but occupied a key position geographically. It was in these states that the Federalists waged their most aggressive campaigns.

In Massachusetts, where the ratifying convention was summoned for January, the Federalists were fortunate in having most of the political talent in the state on their side. The two men who might have led the opposition, Samuel Adams and Elbridge Gerry, played minor roles: Adams sensed that his constituency, Boston, favored the new instrument and he did not care to go against the town; Gerry, who had participated actively in framing the Constitution, was unwilling to assume an active hostility to it, even though he had refused to sign it. When the convention met, however, the anti-Federalists seemed to be in the majority. The Federalists saw that their only chance was to talk the delegates around.

This was no easy task, for many had been specifically instructed by their constituents to reject the document. What finally saved the day was the conversion of John Hancock, who had been chosen presiding officer of the convention. Hancock had great prestige as a Revolutionary patriot, but his attitude toward the Constitution was at first undecided, and a touch of the gout kept him away from the initial meetings. Among those who knew him well, Hancock had the reputation of a weathercock, and Rufus King uncharitably observed of his absence that "as soon as the majority is exhibited on either Side I think his Health will suffice him to be abroad." To hasten his recovery, however, the Federalists offered to support him in the next gubernatorial election if he would support them now. It was even suggested that he was the obvious candidate for the Vice-Presidency under the new government, and if Virginia did not ratify (which would disqualify Washington)—well, who could tell. . .?

The Federalist medicine worked, and Hancock at last appeared at

the convention, a plan of accommodation in hand. He proposed
that they ratify the Constitution but at the same time recommend
the immediate adoption of a set of amendments which would
remove most of the objections to it. This formula won over enough
of the opposition to secure ratification on February 6, 1788, by a
vote of 187 to 168.

It was a narrow squeak, but it helped greatly to swing hesitating
states into line. Not only did acceptance by Massachusetts carry
weight with the skeptical, but the formula of unconditional
ratification with recommended amendments proved a fruitful one
in later conventions. Maryland ratified unconditionally in April and
South Carolina in May with recommendations for amendment.

Virginia was next, and her decision would be crucial. She was the
largest state in the union; she had played almost as prominent a
part in the Revolution as Massachusetts; and she had the most
distinguished statesmen in the country. The talents of Washington,
Jefferson, and Madison, to mention only a few, would be sadly
missed by the nation if Virginia refused to join the union. The
ratifying convention was set for June, 1788, at Richmond, and as
the date approached there was an uncomfortably strong public
sentiment in opposition. Two of the state's delegates to the
Philadelphia convention, George Mason and Edmund Randolph,
had refused to sign the Constitution because they thought it
contained insufficient safeguards for popular liberties, and their
opinions carried much weight. Patrick Henry, whose influence was
enormous, had of course refused to attend at Philadelphia and was
thundering in self-righteous indignation at what went on there. He
and Mason and Randolph would all be at Richmond and were
expected to present a formidable barrier to ratification.

Fortunately for the Federalists, however, the greatest of Virginia's
political giants were with them, and they kept the contest pitched

at a higher level than in any other state. Though Washington declined to serve in the ratifying convention, he was known to favor adoption. George Wythe was for it; Madison was for it; Edmund Pendleton was for it, and so revered by his neighbors that they sent him to the convention even though they were against the Constitution themselves. When the delegates assembled at Richmond, Henry's assault was met by a formidable counterattack, in which to his consternation Randolph joined. Randolph's opposition had always been mild. He had wanted amendments to be suggested by the states and these to be sifted by a new convention. Now, however, he stood up and announced that too much time had passed to make this safe. He was ready to vote "Yes" and follow the Massachusetts procedure of unconditional ratification with recommended amendments. In spite of Randolph's assistance the Federalists found it rough sledding, but in the end they carried the day eighty-nine to seventy-nine.

With ratification by Virginia and by New Hampshire (which came in under the Massachusetts formula while the Virginia convention was in progress), the union was assured of ten members, one more than was needed to put the new government in operation. New York followed almost at once. The ratifying convention there had initially shown a large majority against the Constitution, but the Federalists, led by Alexander Hamilton, had convinced their opponents by a combination of threats (that New York City and the adjacent counties would secede from the rest of the state in order to join the union) and promises (of support for numerous amendments).

Only North Carolina and Rhode Island remained, but the Philadelphia convention had anticipated that some states might balk. That Rhode Island should be one of the recalcitrants served to confirm the somewhat slanderous phrases that had been uttered about her at Philadelphia and subsequently in most of the ratifying conventions. It took North Carolina until November, 1789, and Rhode Island until May, 1790, to join the rest of the United States under the usual formula of recommended amendments.

In spite of the bitter fights that preceded ratification, the differences between Federalists and anti-Federalists were primarily differences of opinion about means, not fundamental differences of principle. Both sides wanted an effective national government. Both sides wanted to guard that government against tyranny. Their disagreement was over the question whether the proposed separation of powers would be an adequate guard. The anti-Federalists thought not, and the amendments they recommended were digested by James Madison (who was also the principal author of the Constitution itself) to become the first ten amendments, usually called the Bill of Rights. These amendments in no way threatened the workability of the new government. Had Madison and his friends had the foresight to include them in the original document, ratification would have been much easier. Instead, it was obtained by the narrowest of margins and by methods that cannot be defended.

The result achieved was so happy that for a century or more these methods were forgotten, and the founding fathers escaped serious criticism. The present century has looked upon the vilification, the pressure, and the politicking, and has sometimes condemned not only the methods but, by implication at least, the result. The Constitution, it has been suggested, represented a reaction from the democratic principles of the Revolution, a reaction engineered by the rich and well-born, which was only overcome by the Jeffersonian and Jacksonian movements that followed.

Everyone who studies the Revolution and the Constitution must decide for himself whether this was true. It is worth pointing out, however, that if the Revolution was a struggle to make property secure, the Constitution was the final fulfilment of the struggle. If the Revolution called for the coupling of taxation with representation, the Constitution made the central government representative before giving it powers to tax. If the Revolution was built upon the principle that all men are created equal, the Constitution gave men a more equal share in the national government than the Confederation did. If the Revolution opened for Americans the discovery of their own nationality, the Constitution gave them the instrument for expressing it. If the Revolution taught them the danger of tyranny, the aim of the Constitution was to prevent tyranny.

Most of us will think it was successful. But the men who made it knew it was not the end of the search. They had come a long way in twenty-five years, perhaps as far as men have ever come in so short a time, but the farther they traveled, the fairer the prospect that lay ahead. The Constitution was a bulwark to protect what they had gained, but it was also a base from which to continue the exploration. The bulwark still stands, and in spite of halts and pauses along the way the exploration still goes on. As long as any man remains less free than another, it cannot honorably cease.

Appendix
Basic Documents of the Revolution

THE DECLARATION OF INDEPENDENCE
In Congress, July 4, 1776
THE UNANIMOUS DECLARATION OF THE THIRTEEN
UNITED STATES OF AMERICA

When in the Course of human events, it becomes necessary for one people to dissolve the political bands which have connected them with another, and to assume among the powers of the earth, the separate and equal station to which the Laws of Nature and of Nature's God entitle them, a decent respect to the opinions of mankind requires that they should declare the causes which impel them to the separation.—We hold these truths to be self-evident, that all men are created equal, that they are endowed by their Creator with certain unalienable Rights, that among these are Life, Liberty and the pursuit of Happiness.—That to secure these rights, Governments are instituted among Men, deriving their just powers from the consent of the governed.—That whenever any Form of Government becomes destructive of these ends, it is the Right of the People to alter or to abolish it, and to institute new Government, laying its foundation on such principles and organizing its powers in such form, as to them shall seem most likely to effect their Safety and Happiness. Prudence, indeed, will dictate that Governments long established should not be changed for light and transient causes; and accordingly all experience hath shown, that mankind are more disposed to suffer, while evils are sufferable, than to right themselves by abolishing the forms to which they are accustomed. But when a long train of abuses and usurpations, pursuing invariably the same Object evinces a design to reduce them under absolute Despotism, it is their right, it is their duty, to throw off such Government, and to provide new Guards for their future security.—Such has been the patient sufferance of these Colonies; and such is now the necessity which constrains them to alter their former Systems of Government. The history of the present King of Great Britain is a history of repeated injuries and usurpations, all having in direct object the establishment of an absolute Tyranny over these States. To prove this, let Facts be submitted to a candid world.—He has refused his Assent to Laws, the most wholesome and necessary for the public good.—He has forbidden his Governors to pass Laws of

Printed from the facsimile of the engrossed copy of the original manuscript in the Library of Congress.

Appendix

immediate and pressing importance, unless suspended in their operation till his Assent should be obtained; and when so suspended, he has utterly neglected to attend to them.—He has refused to pass other Laws for the accommodation of large districts of people, unless those people would relinquish the right of Representation in the Legislature, a right inestimable to them and formidable to tyrants only.—He has called together legislative bodies at places unusual, uncomfortable, and distant from the depository of their public Records, for the sole purpose of fatiguing them into compliance with his measures.—He has dissolved Representative Houses repeatedly, for opposing with manly firmness his invasions on the rights of the people.—He has refused for a long time, after such dissolutions, to cause others to be elected; whereby the Legislative powers, incapable of Annihilation, have returned to the People at large for their exercise; the State remaining in the mean time exposed to all the dangers of invasion from without, and convulsions within.—He has endeavoured to prevent the population of these States; for that purpose obstructing the Laws for Naturalization of Foreigners; refusing to pass others to encourage their migration hither, and raising the conditions of new Appropriations of Lands.—He has obstructed the Administration of Justice, by refusing his Assent to Laws for establishing Judiciary powers. —He has made Judges dependent on his Will alone, for the tenure of their offices, and the amount and payment of their salaries.—He has erected a multitude of New Offices, and sent hither swarms of Officers to harrass our people, and eat out their substance.—He has kept among us, in times of peace, Standing Armies, without the Consent of our legislatures.—He has affected to render the Military independent of and superior to the Civil power.—He has combined with others to subject us to a jurisdiction foreign to our constitution, and unacknowledged by our laws; giving his Assent to their Acts of pretended Legislation:—For quartering large bodies of armed troops among us:—For protecting them, by a mock Trial, from punishment for any Murders which they should commit on the Inhabitants of these States:—For cutting off our Trade with all parts of the world:—For imposing Taxes on us without our Consent:—For depriving us in many cases, of the benefits of Trial by Jury:—For transporting us beyond Seas to be tried for pretended offences:—For abolishing the free System of English Laws in a neighbouring Province, establishing therein an Arbitrary government, and enlarging its Boundaries so as to render it at once an example and fit instrument for introducing the same absolute rule into these Colonies:—For taking away our Charters, abolishing our most valuable

The Declaration of Independence

Laws, and altering fundamentally the Forms of our Governments:—For suspending our own Legislatures, and declaring themselves invested with power to legislate for us in all cases whatsoever.—He has abdicated Government here, by declaring us out of his Protection and waging War against us.—He has plundered our seas, ravaged our Coasts, burnt our towns, and destroyed the lives of our people.—He is at this time transporting large Armies of foreign Mercenaries to compleat the works of death, desolation and tyranny, already begun with circumstances of Cruelty & perfidy scarcely paralleled in the most barbarous ages, and totally unworthy the Head of a civilized nation.—He has constrained our fellow Citizens taken Captive on the high Seas to bear Arms against their Country, to become the executioners of their friends and Brethren, or to fall themselves by their Hands.—He has excited domestic insurrections amongst us, and has endeavoured to bring on the inhabitants of our frontiers, the merciless Indian Savages, whose known rule of warfare, is an undistinguished destruction of all ages, sexes and conditions. In every stage of these Oppressions We have Petitioned for Redress in the most humble terms: Our repeated Petitions have been answered only by repeated injury. A Prince, whose character is thus marked by every act which may define a Tyrant, is unfit to be the ruler of a free people. Nor have We been wanting in attentions to our Brittish brethren. We have warned them from time to time of attempts by their legislature to extend an unwarrantable jurisdiction over us. We have reminded them of the circumstances of our emigration and settlement here. We have appealed to their native justice and magnanimity, and we have conjured them by the ties of our common kindred to disavow these usurpations, which, would inevitably interrupt our connections and correspondence. They too have been deaf to the voice of justice and of consanguinity. We must, therefore, acquiesce in the necessity, which denounces our Separation, and hold them, as we hold the rest of mankind, Enemies in War, in Peace Friends.—

WE, THEREFORE, the REPRESENTATIVES of the UNITED STATES OF AMERICA, in General Congress, Assembled, appealing to the Supreme Judge of the world for the rectitude of our intentions, do, in the Name, and by Authority of the good People of these Colonies, solemnly publish and declare, That these United Colonies are, and of Right ought to be FREE AND INDEPENDENT STATES; that they are Absolved from all Allegiance to the British Crown, and that all political connection between them and the State of Great Britain, is and ought to be totally dissolved; and that as Free and Independent States, they have full Power to levy War, conclude Peace,

Appendix

contract Alliances, establish Commerce, and to do all other Acts and Things which Independent States may of right do.—And for the support of this Declaration, with a firm reliance on the protection of Divine Providence, we mutually pledge to each other our Lives, our Fortunes and our sacred Honor.

[Signatures omitted]

ARTICLES OF CONFEDERATION,
March 1, 1781

To all to whom these Presents shall come, we the under signed Delegates of the States affixed to our Names, send greeting.

Whereas the Delegates of the United States of America, in Congress assembled, did, on the 15th day of November, in the Year of Our Lord One thousand Seven Hundred and Seventy seven, and in the Second Year of the Independence of America, agree to certain articles of Confederation and perpetual Union between the States of Newhampshire, Massachusetts-bay, Rhodeisland and Providence Plantations, Connecticut, New York, New Jersey, Pennsylvania, Delaware, Maryland, Virginia, North-Carolina, South-Carolina, and Georgia in the words following, viz. "Articles of Confederation and perpetual Union between the states of Newhampshire, Massachusetts-bay, Rhodeisland and Providence Plantations, Connecticut, New-York, New-Jersey, Pennsylvania, Delaware, Maryland, Virginia, North-Carolina, South-Carolina and Georgia.

ARTICLE I. The Stile of this confederacy shall be "The United States of America."

ARTICLE II. Each state retains its sovereignty, freedom, and independence, and every Power, Jurisdiction and right, which is not by this confederation expressly delegated to the United States, in Congress assembled.

ARTICLE III. The said states hereby severally enter into a firm league of friendship with each other, for their common defence, the security of their Liberties, and their mutual and general welfare, binding themselves to assist each other, against all force offered to, or attacks made upon them, or any of them, on account of religion, sovereignty, trade, or any other pretence whatever.

ARTICLE IV. The better to secure and perpetuate mutual friendship and intercourse among the people of the different states in this union, the free inhabitants of each of these states, paupers, vagabonds and fugitives from justice excepted, shall be entitled to all privileges and immunities of free citizens in the several states; and the people of each state shall have free ingress and regress to and from any other state, and shall enjoy therein all the privileges of trade and commerce, subject to the same duties, impositions and restrictions as the inhabitants thereof respectively, provided that such restriction shall not extend so far as to prevent the

Reprinted from *Journals of the Continental Congress*, Library of Congress edition, XIX (1912), 214.

Appendix

removal of property imported into any state, to any other state, of which the Owner is an inhabitant; provided also that no imposition, duties or restriction shall be laid by any state, on the property of the united states, or either of them.

If any Person guilty of, or charged with treason, felony, or other high misdemeanor in any state, shall flee from Justice, and be found in any of the united states, he shall, upon demand of the Governor or executive power, of the state from which he fled, be delivered up and removed to the state having jurisdiction of his offence.

Full faith and credit shall be given in each of these states to the records, acts and judicial proceedings of the courts and magistrates of every other state.

ARTICLE V. For the more convenient management of the general interests of the united states, delegates shall be annually appointed in such manner as the legislature of each state shall direct, to meet in Congress on the first Monday in November, in every year, with a power reserved to each state, to recal its delegates, or any of them, at any time within the year, and to send others in their stead, for the remainder of the Year.

No state shall be represented in Congress by less than two, nor by more than seven Members; and no person shall be capable of being a delegate for more than three years in any term of six years; nor shall any person, being a delegate, be capable of holding any office under the united states, for which he, or another for his benefit receives any salary, fees or emolument of any kind.

Each state shall maintain its own delegates in a meeting of the states, and while they act as members of the committee of the states.

In determining questions in the united states in Congress assembled, each state shall have one vote.

Freedom of speech and debate in Congress shall not be impeached or questioned in any Court, or place out of Congress, and the members of congress shall be protected in their persons from arrests and imprisonments, during the time of their going to and from, and attendance on congress, except for treason, felony, or breach of the peace.

ARTICLE VI. No state, without the Consent of the united states in congress assembled, shall send any embassy to, or receive any embassy from, or enter into any conference, agreement, alliance or treaty with any King, prince or state; nor shall any person holding any office of profit or trust under the united states, or any of them, accept of any present, emolument, office or title of any kind whatever from any king, prince or

164

foreign state; nor shall the united states in congress assembled, or any of them, grant any title of nobility.

No two or more states shall enter into any treaty, confederation or alliance whatever between them, without the consent of the united states in congress assembled, specifying accurately the purposes for which the same is to be entered into, and how long it shall continue.

No state shall lay any imposts or duties, which may interfere with any stipulations in treaties, entered into by the united states in congress assembled, with any king, prince or state, in pursuance of any treaties already proposed by congress, to the courts of France and Spain.

No vessels of war shall be kept up in time of peace by any state, except such number only, as shall be deemed necessary by the united states in congress assembled, for the defence of such state, or its trade; nor shall any body of forces be kept up by any state, in time of peace, except such number only, as in the judgment of the united states, in congress assembled, shall be deemed requisite to garrison the forts necessary for the defence of such state; but every state shall always keep up a well regulated and disciplined militia, sufficiently armed and accoutred, and shall provide and constantly have ready for use, in public stores, a due number of field pieces and tents, and a proper quantity of arms, ammunition and camp equipage.

No state shall engage in any war without the consent of the united states in congress assembled, unless such state be actually invaded by enemies, or shall have received certain advice of a resolution being formed by some nation of Indians to invade such state, and the danger is so imminent as not to admit of a delay till the united states in congress assembled can be consulted: nor shall any state grant commissions to any ships or vessels of war, nor letters of marque or reprisal, except it be after a declaration of war by the united states in congress assembled, and then only against the kingdom or state and the subjects thereof, against which war has been so declared, and under such regulations as shall be established by the united states in congress assembled, unless such state be infested by pirates, in which case vessels of war may be fitted out for that occasion, and kept so long as the danger shall continue, or until the united states in congress assembled shall determine otherwise.

ARTICLE VII. When land-forces are raised by any state for the common defence, all officers of or under the rank of colonel, shall be appointed by the legislature of each state respectively, by whom such forces shall be raised, or in such manner as such state shall direct, and all vacancies shall be filled up by the State which first made the appointment.

Appendix

ARTICLE VIII. All charges of war, and all other expences that shall be incurred for the common defence or general welfare, and allowed by the united states in congress assembled, shall be defrayed out of a common treasury, which shall be supplied by the several states in proportion to the value of all land within each state, granted to or surveyed for any Person, as such land and the buildings and improvements thereon shall be estimated according to such mode as the united states in congress assembled, shall from time to time direct and appoint.

The taxes for paying that proportion shall be laid and levied by the authority and direction of the legislatures of the several states within the time agreed upon by the united states in congress assembled.

ARTICLE IX. The united states in congress assembled, shall have the sole and exclusive right and power of determining on peace and war, except in the cases mentioned in the sixth article—of sending and receiving ambassadors—entering into treaties and alliances, provided that no treaty of commerce shall be made whereby the legislative power of the respective states shall be restrained from imposing such imposts and duties on foreigners as their own people are subjected to, or from prohibiting the exportation or importation of any species of goods or commodities, whatsoever—of establishing rules for deciding in all cases, what captures on land or water shall be legal, and in what manner prizes taken by land or naval forces in the service of the united states shall be divided or appropriated—of granting letters of marque and reprisal in times of peace—appointing courts for the trial of piracies and felonies committed on the high seas and establishing courts for receiving and determining finally appeals in all cases of captures, provided that no member of congress shall be appointed a judge of any of the said courts.

The united states in congress assembled shall also be the last resort on appeal in all disputes and differences now subsisting or that hereafter may arise between two or more states concerning boundary, jurisdiction or any other cause whatever; which authority shall always be exercised in the manner following. Whenever the legislative or executive authority or lawful agent of any state in controversy with another shall present a petition to congress stating the matter in question and praying for a hearing, notice thereof shall be given by order of congress to the legislative or executive authority of the other state in controversy, and a day assigned for the appearance of the parties by their lawful agents, who shall then be directed to appoint by joint consent, commissioners or judges to constitute a court for hearing and determining the matter in question: but if they

166

cannot agree, congress shall name three persons out of each of the united states, and from the list of such persons each party shall alternately strike out one, the petitioners beginning, until the number shall be reduced to thirteen; and from that number not less than seven, nor more than nine names as congress shall direct, shall in the presence of congress be drawn out by lot, and the persons whose names shall be so drawn or any five of them, shall be commissioners or judges, to hear and finally determine the controversy, so always as a major part of the judges who shall hear the cause shall agree in the determination: and if either party shall neglect to attend at the day appointed, without showing reasons, which congress shall judge sufficient, or being present shall refuse to strike, the congress shall proceed to nominate three persons out of each state, and the secretary of congress shall strike in behalf of such party absent or refusing; and the judgment and sentence of the court to be appointed, in the manner before prescribed, shall be final and conclusive; and if any of the parties shall refuse to submit to the authority of such court, or to appear or defend their claim or cause, the court shall nevertheless proceed to pronounce sentence, or judgment, which shall in like manner be final and decisive, the judgment or sentence and other proceedings being in either case transmitted to congress, and lodged among the acts of congress for the security of the parties concerned: provided that every commissioner, before he sits in judgment, shall take an oath to be administered by one of the judges of the supreme or superior court of the state, where the cause shall be tried, "well and truly to hear and determine the matter in question, according to the best of his judgment, without favour, affection or hope of reward:" provided also, that no state shall be deprived of territory for the benefit of the united states.

All controversies concerning the private right of soil claimed under different grants of two or more states, whose jurisdictions as they may respect such lands, and the states which passed such grants are adjusted, the said grants or either of them being at the same time claimed to have originated antecedent to such settlement of jurisdiction, shall on the petition of either party to the congress of the united states, be finally determined as near as may be in the same manner as is before prescribed for deciding disputes respecting territorial jurisidiction between different states.

The united states in congress assembled shall also have the sole and exclusive right and power of regulating the alloy and value of coin struck by their own authority, or by that of the respective states—fixing the standard

Appendix

of weights and measures throughout the united states—regulating the trade and managing all affairs with the Indians, not members of any of the states, provided that the legislative right of any state within its own limits be not infringed or violated—establishing or regulating post-offices from one state to another, throughout all the united states, and exacting such postage on the papers passing thro' the same as may be requisite to defray the expences of the said office—appointing all officers of the land forces, in the service of the united states, excepting regimental officers—appointing all the officers of the naval forces, and commissioning all officers whatever in the service of the united states—making rules for the government and regulation of the said land and naval forces, and directing their operations.

The united states in congress assembled shall have authority to appoint a committee, to sit in the recess of congress, to be denominated "A Committee of the States," and to consist of one delegate from each state; and to appoint such other committees and civil officers as may be necessary for managing the general affairs of the united states under their direction—to appoint one of their number to preside, provided that no person be allowed to serve in the office of president more than one year in any term of three years; to ascertain the necessary sums of money to be raised for the service of the united states, and to appropriate and apply the same for defraying the public expences—to borrow money, or emit bills on the credit of the united states, transmitting every half year to the respective states an account of the sums of money so borrowed or emitted,—to build and equip a navy—to agree upon the number of land forces, and to make requisitions from each state for its quota, in proportion to the number of white inhabitants in such state; which requisition shall be binding, and thereupon the legislature of each state shall appoint the regimental officers, raise the men and cloath, arm and equip them in a soldier like manner, at the expence of the united states; and the officers and men so cloathed, armed and equipped shall march to the place appointed, and within the time agreed on by the united states in congress assembled: But if the united states in congress assembled shall, on consideration of circumstances judge proper that any state should not raise men, or should raise a smaller number than its quota, and that any other state should raise a greater number of men than the quota thereof, such extra number shall be raised, officered, cloathed, armed and equipped in the same manner as the quota of such state, unless the legislature of such state shall judge that such extra number cannot be safely spared out of the same, in which case they shall raise officer, cloath, arm and equip as many of such extra number as they judge can be safely spared. And the officers and men so cloathed, armed and equipped, shall march to the place appointed, and within the time agreed on by the united states in congress assembled.

The united states in congress assembled shall never engage in a war, nor grant letters of marque and reprisal in time of peace, nor enter into any treaties or alliances, nor coin money, nor regulate the value thereof, nor ascertain the sums and expences necessary for the defence and welfare of the united states, or any of them, nor emit bills, nor borrow money on the credit of the united states, nor appropriate money, nor agree upon the number of vessels of war, to be built or purchased, or the number of land or sea forces to be raised, nor appoint a commander in chief of the army or navy, unless nine states assent to the same: nor shall a question on any other point, except for adjourning from day to day be determined, unless by the votes of a majority of the united states in congress assembled.

The congress of the united states shall have power to adjourn to any time within the year, and to any place within the united states, so that no period of adjournment be for a longer duration than the space of six Months, and shall publish the Journal of their proceedings monthly, except such parts thereof relating to treaties, alliances or military operations, as in their judgment require secrecy; and the yeas and nays of the delegates of each state on any question shall be entered on the Journal, when it is desired by any delegate; and the delegates of a state, or any of them, at his or their request shall be furnished with a transcript of the said Journal, except such parts as are above excepted, to lay before the legislatures of the several states.

ARTICLE X. The committee of the states, or any nine of them, shall be authorized to execute, in the recess of congress, such of the powers of congress as the united states in congress assembled, by the consent of nine states, shall from time to time think expedient to vest them with; provided that no power be delegated to the said committee, for the exercise of which, by the articles of confederation, the voice of nine states in the congress of the united states assembled is requisite.

ARTICLE XI. Canada acceding to this confederation, and joining in the measures of the united states, shall be admitted into, and entitled to all the advantages of this union: but no other colony shall be admitted into the same, unless such admission be agreed to by nine states.

ARTICLE XII. All bills of credit emitted, monies borrowed and debts contracted by, or under the authority of congress, before the assembling of the united states, in pursuance of the present confederation, shall be deemed and considered as a charge against the united states, for payment and satisfaction whereof the said united states, and the public faith are hereby solemnly pledged.

ARTICLE XIII. Every state shall abide by the determinations of the united states in congress assembled, on all questions which by this confederation are submitted to them. And the Articles of this confederation shall be inviolably observed by every state, and the union shall be perpetual; nor shall any alteration at any time hereafter be made in any of them; unless such alteration be agreed to in a congress of the united states, and be afterwards confirmed by the legislatures of every state.

And Whereas it hath pleased the Great Governor of the World to incline the hearts of the legislatures we respectively represent in congress, to approve of, and to authorize us to ratify the said articles of confederation and perpetual union. Know Ye that we the undersigned delegates, by virtue of the power and authority to us given for that purpose, do by these presents, in the name and in behalf of our respective constituents, fully and entirely ratify and confirm each and every of the said articles of confederation and perpetual union, and all and singular the matters and things therein contained: And we do further solemnly plight and engage the faith of our respective constituents, that they shall abide by the determinations of the united states in congress assembled, on all questions, which by the said confederation are submitted to them. And that the articles thereof shall be inviolably observed by the states we respectively represent, and that the union shall be perpetual. In Witness whereof we have hereunto set our hands in Congress. Done at Philadelphia in the state of Pennsylvania the ninth day of July, in the Year of our Lord one Thousand seven Hundred and Seventy-eight, and in the third year of the independence of America.

[Signatures omitted]

THE CONSTITUTION OF THE UNITED STATES

We the People of the United States, in Order to form a more perfect Union, establish Justice, insure domestic Tranquility, provide for the common defence, promote the general Welfare, and secure the Blessings of Liberty to ourselves and our Posterity, do ordain and establish this Constitution for the United States of America.

ARTICLE. I.

Section. I.   All legislative Powers herein granted shall be vested in a Congress of the United States, which shall consist of a Senate and House of Representatives.

Section. 2.   The House of Representatives shall be composed of Members chosen every second Year by the People of the several States, and the Electors in each State shall have the Qualifications requisite for Electors of the most numerous Branch of the State Legislature.

No person shall be a Representative who shall not have attained to the Age of twenty five Years, and been seven Years a Citizen of the United States, and who shall not, when elected, be an Inhabitant of that State in which he shall be chosen.

Representatives and direct Taxes shall be apportioned among the several States which may be included within this Union, according to their respective Numbers, which shall be determined by adding to the whole Number of free Persons, including those bound to Service for a Term of Years, and excluding Indians not taxed, three fifths of all other Persons. The actual Enumeration shall be made within three Years after the first Meeting of the Congress of the United States, and within every subsequent Term of ten Years, in such Manner as they shall by Law direct. The Number of Representatives shall not exceed one for every thirty Thousand, but each State shall have at Least one Representative; and until such enumeration shall be made, the State of New Hampshire shall be entitled to chuse three, Massachusetts eight, Rhode Island and Providence Plantations one, Connecticut five, New York six, New Jersey four, Pennsylvania eight, Delaware one, Maryland six, Virginia ten, North Carolina five, South Carolina five, and Georgia three.

When vacancies happen in the Representation from any State, the Executive Authority thereof shall issue Writs of Election to fill such Vacancies.

This is a literal copy of the engrossed Constitution as signed. It is in four sheets, with an additional sheet containing the resolutions of transmittal.

Appendix

The House of Representatives shall chuse their Speaker and other Officers; and shall have the sole Power of Impeachment.

Section. 3. The Senate of the United States shall be composed of two Senators from each State, chosen by the Legislature thereof, for six Years; and each Senator shall have one Vote.

Immediately after they shall be assembled in Consequence of the first Election, they shall be divided as equally as may be into three Classes. The Seats of the Senators of the first Class shall be vacated at the Expiration of the second Year, of the second Class at the Expiration of the fourth Year, and of the third Class at the Expiration of the sixth Year, so that one third may be chosen every second Year; and if Vacancies happen by Resignation, or otherwise, during the Recess of the Legislature of any State, the Executive thereof may make temporary Appointments until the next Meeting of the Legislature, which shall then fill such Vacancies.

No Person shall be a Senator who shall not have attained to the Age of thirty Years, and been nine Years a Citizen of the United States, and who shall not, when elected, be an Inhabitant of that State for which he shall be chosen.

The Vice President of the United States shall be President of the Senate, but shall have no Vote, unless they be equally divided.

The Senate shall chuse their other Officers, and also a President pro tempore, in the Absence of the Vice President, or when he shall exercise the Office of President of the United States.

The Senate shall have the sole Power to try all Impeachments. When sitting for that Purpose, they shall be on Oath or Affirmation. When the president of the United States is tried, the Chief Justice shall preside: And no Person shall be convicted without the Concurrence of two thirds of the Members present.

Judgment in Cases of Impeachment shall not extend further than to removal from Office, and disqualification to hold and enjoy any Office of honor, Trust or Profit under the United States: but the Party convicted shall nevertheless be liable and subject to Indictment, Trial, Judgment and Punishment, according to Law.

Section. 4. The Times, Places and Manner of holding Elections for Senators and Representatives, shall be prescribed in each State by the Legislature thereof; but the Congress may at any time by Law make or alter such Regulations, except as to the Places of chusing Senators.

The Congress shall assemble at least once in every Year, and such Meeting shall be on the first Monday in December, unless they shall by Law appoint a different Day.

Section. 5. Each House shall be the Judge of the Elections, Returns and Qualifications of its own Members, and a Majority of each shall constitute a Quorum to do Business; but a smaller Number may adjourn from day to day, and may be authorized to compel the Attendance of absent Members, in such Manner, and under such Penalties as each House may provide.

Each House may determine the Rules of its Proceedings, punish its Members for disorderly Behaviour, and, with the Concurrence of two thirds, expel a Member.

Each House shall keep a Journal of its Proceedings, and from time to time publish the same, excepting such Parts as may in their Judgment require Secrecy; and the Yeas and Nays of the Members of either House on any question shall, at the Desire of one fifth of those Present, be entered on the Journal.

Neither House, during the Session of Congress, shall, without the Consent of the other, adjourn for more than three days, nor to any other Place than that in which the two Houses shall be sitting.

Section. 6. The Senators and Representatives shall receive a Compensation for their Services, to be ascertained by Law, and paid out of the Treasury of the United States. They shall in all Cases, except Treason, Felony and Breach of the Peace, be privileged from Arrest during their Attendance at the Session of their respective Houses, and in going to and returning from the same; and for any Speech or Debate in either House, they shall not be questioned in any other Place.

No Senator or Representative shall, during the Time for which he was elected, be appointed to any civil Office under the Authority of the United States, which shall have been created, or the Emoluments whereof shall have been encreased during such time; and no Person holding any Office under the United States, shall be a Member of either House during his Continuance in Office.

Section. 7. All Bills for raising Revenue shall originate in the House of Representatives; but the Senate may propose or concur with Amendments as on other Bills.

Every Bill which shall have passed the House of Representatives and the Senate, shall, before it become a Law, be presented to the President of the United States; If he approve he shall sign it, but if not he shall return it, with his Objections to that House in which it shall have originated, who shall enter the Objections at large on their Journal, and proceed to reconsider it. If after such Reconsideration two thirds of that House shall agree to pass the Bill, it shall be sent, together with the Objections, to the other House, by which it shall likewise be reconsidered, and if approved by

Appendix

two thirds of that House, it shall become a Law. But in all such Cases the Votes of both Houses shall be determined by yeas and Nays, and the Names of the Persons voting for and against the Bill shall be entered on the Journal of each House respectively. If any Bill shall not be returned by the President within ten days (Sundays excepted) after it shall have been presented to him, the Same shall be a Law, in like Manner as if he had signed it, unless the Congress by their Adjournment prevent its Return in which Case it shall not be a Law.

Every Order, Resolution, or Vote to which the Concurrence of the Senate and House of Representatives may be necessary (except on a question of Adjournment) shall be presented to the President of the United States; and before the Same shall take Effect, shall be approved by him, or being disapproved by him, shall be repassed by two thirds of the Senate and House of Representatives, according to the Rules and Limitations prescribed in the Case of a Bill.

Section. 8. The Congress shall have Power To lay and collect Taxes, Duties, Imposts and Excises, to pay the Debts and provide for the common Defence and general Welfare of the United States; but all Duties, Imposts and Excises shall be uniform throughout the United States;

To borrow Money on the credit of the United States;

To regulate Commerce with foreign Nations, and among the several States, and with the Indian Tribes;

To establish an uniform Rule of Naturalization, and uniform Laws on the subject of Bankruptcies throughout the United States;

To coin Money, regulate the Value thereof, and of foreign Coin, and fix the Standard of Weights and Measures;

To provide for the Punishment of counterfeiting the Securities and current Coin of the United States;

To establish Post Offices and post Roads;

To promote the Progress of Science and useful Arts, by securing for limited Times to Authors and Inventors the exclusive Right to their respective Writings and Discoveries;

To constitute Tribunals inferior to the supreme Court;

To define and punish Piracies and Felonies committed on the high Seas, and Offences against the Law of Nations;

To declare War, grant Letters of Marque and Reprisal, and make Rules concerning Captures on Land and Water;

To raise and support Armies, but no Appropriation of Money to that Use shall be for a longer Term than two Years;

To provide and maintain a Navy;

To make Rules for the Government and Regulation of the land and naval Forces;

To provide for calling forth the Militia to execute the Laws of the Union, suppress Insurrections and repel Invasions;

To provide for organizing, arming, and disciplining, the Militia, and for governing such Part of them as may be employed in the Service of the United States, reserving to the States respectively, the Appointment of the Officers, and the Authority of training the Militia according to the discipline prescribed by Congress;

To exercise exclusive Legislation in all Cases whatsoever, over such District (not exceeding ten Miles square) as may, by Cession of particular States, and the Acceptance of Congress, become the Seat of the Government of the United States, and to exercise like Authority over all Places purchased by the Consent of the Legislature of the State in which the Same shall be, for the Erection of Forts, Magazines, Arsenals, dock-Yards, and other needful Buildings;—And

To make all Laws which shall be necessary and proper for carrying into Execution the foregoing Powers, and all other Powers vested by this Constitution in the Government of the United States, or in any Department or Officer thereof.

Section. 9.   The Migration or Importation of such Persons as any of the States now existing shall think proper to admit, shall not be prohibited by the Congress prior to the Year one thousand eight hundred and eight, but a Tax or duty may be imposed on such Importation, not exceeding ten dollars for each Person.

The Privilege of the Writ of Habeas Corpus shall not be suspended, unless when in Cases of Rebellion or Invasion the public Safety may require it.

No Bill of Attainder or ex post facto Law shall be passed.

No Capitation, or other direct, Tax shall be laid, unless in Proportion to the Census or Enumeration herein before directed to be taken.

No Tax or Duty shall be laid on Articles exported from any State.

No Preference shall be given by any Regulation of Commerce or Revenue to the Ports of one State over those of another: nor shall Vessels bound to, or from, one State, be obliged to enter, clear, or pay Duties in another.

No Money shall be drawn from the Treasury, but in Consequence of Appropriations made by Law; and a regular Statement and Account of the Receipts and Expenditures of all public Money shall be published from time to time.

Appendix

No Title of Nobility shall be granted by the United States: And no Person holding any Office of Profit or Trust under them, shall, without the Consent of the Congress, accept of any present, Emolument, Office, or Title, of any kind whatever, from any King, Prince, or foreign State.

Section. 10.   No State shall enter into any Treaty, Alliance, or Confederation; grant Letters of Marque and Reprisal; coin Money; emit Bills of Credit; make any Thing but gold and silver Coin a Tender in Payment of Debts; pass any Bill of Attainder, ex post facto Law, or Law impairing the Obligation of Contracts, or grant any Title of Nobility.

No State shall, without the Consent of the Congress, lay any Imposts or Duties on Imports or Exports, except what may be absolutely necessary for executing its inspection Laws: and the net Produce of all Duties and Imposts, laid by any State on Imports or Exports, shall be for the Use of the Treasury of the United States; and all such Laws shall be subject to the Revision and Controul of the Congress.

No State shall, without the Consent of Congress, lay any Duty of Tonnage, keep Troops, or Ships of War in time of Peace, enter into any Agreement or Compact with another State, or with a foreign Power, or engage in War, unless actually invaded, or in such imminent Danger as will not admit of delay.

ARTICLE. II.

Section. I.   The executive Power shall be vested in a President of the United States of America. He shall hold his Office during the Term of four Years, and, together with the Vice President, chosen for the same Term, be elected as follows

Each State shall appoint, in such Manner as the Legislature thereof may direct, a Number of Electors, equal to the whole Number of Senators and Representatives to which the State may be entitled in the Congress: but no Senator or Representative, or Person holding an Office of Trust or Profit under the United States, shall be appointed an Elector.

The Electors shall meet in their respective States, and vote by Ballot for two Persons, of whom one at least shall not be an Inhabitant of the same State with themselves. And they shall make a List of all the Persons voted for, and of the Number of Votes for each; which List they shall sign and certify, and transmit sealed to the Seat of the Government of the United States, directed to the President of the Senate. The President of the Senate shall, in the Presence of the Senate and House of Representatives, open all the Certificates, and the Votes shall then be counted. The Person having the greatest Number of Votes shall be the President, if such Number be a Majority of the whole Number of Electors appointed; and if there be more than one who have such Majority, and have an equal Number of Votes, then the House of Representatives shall immediately chuse by Ballot one of them for President; and if no Person have a Majority, then from the five highest on the List the said House shall in like Manner chuse the President. But in chusing the President, the Votes shall be taken by States, the Representation from each State having one Vote; A quorum for this Purpose shall consist of a Member or Members from two thirds of the States, and a Majority of all the States shall be necessary to a Choice. In every Case, after the Choice of the President, the Person having the greatest Number of Votes of the Electors shall be the Vice President. But if there should remain two or more who have equal Votes, the Senate shall chuse from them by Ballot the Vice President.

The Congress may determine the Time of chusing the Electors, and the Day on which they shall give their Votes; which Day shall be the same throughout the United States.

No Person except a natural born Citizen, or a Citizen of the United States, at the time of the Adoption of this Constitution, shall be eligible to the Office of President; neither shall any Person be eligible to that Office who shall not have attained to the Age of thirty five Years, and been fourteen Years a Resident within the United States.

In Case of the Removal of the President from Office, or of his Death, Resignation, or Inability to discharge the Powers and Duties of the said Office, the Same shall devolve on the Vice President, and the Congress may by Law provide for the Case of Removal, Death, Resignation or Inability, both of the President and Vice President, declaring what Officer shall then act as President, and such Officer shall act accordingly, until the Disability be removed, or a President shall be elected.

The President shall, at stated Times, receive for his Services, a Compensation, which shall neither be encreased nor diminished during the Period for which he shall have been elected, and he shall not receive within that Period any other Emolument from the United States, or any of them.

Before he enter on the Execution of his Office, he shall take the following Oath or Affirmation:—"I do solemnly swear (or affirm) that I will faithfully execute the Office of President of the United States, and will to the best of my Ability, preserve, protect and defend the Constitution of the United States."

Appendix

Section. 2.   The President shall be Commander in Chief of the Army and Navy of the United States, and of the Militia of the several States, when called into the actual Service of the United States; he may require the Opinion, in writing, of the principal Officer in each of the executive Departments, upon any Subject relating to the Duties of their respective Offices, and he shall have Power to grant Reprieves and Pardons for Offences against the United States, except in Cases of Impeachment.

He shall have Power, by and with the Advice and Consent of the Senate, to make Treaties, provided two thirds of the Senators present concur; and he shall nominate, and by and with the Advice and Consent of the Senate, shall appoint Ambassadors, other public Ministers and Consuls, Judges of the supreme Court, and all other Officers of the United States, whose Appointments are not herein otherwise provided for, and which shall be established by Law: but the Congress may by Law vest the Appointment of such inferior Officers, as they think proper, in the President alone, in the Courts of Law, or in the Heads of Departments.

The President shall have Power to fill up all Vacancies that may happen during the Recess of the Senate, by granting Commissions which shall expire at the End of their next Session.

Section. 3.   He shall from time to time give to the Congress Information of the State of the Union, and recommend to their Consideration such Measures as he shall judge necessary and expedient; he may, on extraordinary Occasions, convene both Houses, or either of them, and in Case of Disagreement between them, with Respect to the Time of Adjournment, he may adjourn them to such Time as he shall think proper; he shall receive Ambassadors and other public Ministers; he shall take Care that the Laws be faithfully executed, and shall Commission all the Officers of the United States.

Section. 4.   The President, Vice President and all civil Officers of the United States, shall be removed from Office on Impeachment for, and Conviction of, Treason, Bribery, or other high Crimes and Misdemeanors.

ARTICLE. III.

Section. I.   The judicial Power of the United States, shall be vested in one supreme Court, and in such inferior Courts as the Congress may from time to time ordain and establish. The Judges, both of the supreme and inferior Courts, shall hold their Offices during good Behaviour, and shall, at stated Times, receive for their Services, a Compensation, which shall not be diminished during their Continuance in Office.

The Constitution of the United States

Section. 2. The judicial Power shall extend to all Cases, in Law and Equity, arising under this Constitution, the Laws of the United States, and Treaties made, or which shall be made, under their Authority;—to all Cases affecting Ambassadors, other public Ministers and Consuls;—to all Cases of admiralty and maritime Jurisdiction;—to Controversies to which the United States shall be a Party;—to Controversies between two or more States;—between a State and Citizens of another State;—between Citizens of different States,—between Citizens of the same State claiming Lands under Grants of different States, and between a State, or the Citizens thereof, and foreign States, Citizens or Subjects.

In all Cases affecting Ambassadors, other public Ministers and Consuls, and those in which a State shall be Party, the supreme Court shall have original Jurisdiction. In all the other Cases before mentioned, the supreme Court shall have appellate Jursidiction, both as to Law and Fact, with such Exceptions, and under such Regulations as the Congress shall make.

The Trial of all Crimes, except in Cases of Impeachment, shall be by Jury; and such Trial shall be held in the State where the said Crimes shall have been committed; but when not committed within any State, the Trial shall be at such Place or Places as the Congress may by Law have directed.

Section. 3. Treason against the United States, shall consist only in levying War against them, or in adhering to their Enemies, giving them Aid and Comfort. No Person shall be convicted of Treason unless on the Testimony of two Witnesses to the same overt Act, or on Confession in open Court.

The Congress shall have Power to declare the Punishment of Treason, but no Attainder of Treason shall work Corruption of Blood, or Forfeiture except during the Life of the Person attainted.

ARTICLE. IV.

Section. I. Full Faith and Credit shall be given in each State to the public Acts, Records, and judicial Proceedings of every other State. And the Congress may by general Laws prescribe the Manner in which such Acts, Records and Proceedings shall be proved, and the Effect thereof.

Section. 2. The Citizens of each State shall be entitled to all Privileges and Immunities of Citizens in the several States.

A Person charged in any State with Treason, Felony, or other Crime, who shall flee from Justice, and be found in another State, shall on Demand of the executive Authority of the State from which he fled, be delivered up, to be removed to the State having Jurisdiction of the Crime.

Appendix

No Person held to Service or Labour in one State, under the Laws thereof, escaping into another, shall, in Consequence of any Law or Regulation therein, be discharged from such Service or Labour, but shall be delivered up on Claim of the Party to whom such Service or Labour may be due.

Section. 3.   New States may be admitted by the Congress into this Union; but no new State shall be formed or erected within the Jurisdiction of any other State; nor any State be formed by the Junction of two or more States, or Parts of States, without the Consent of the Legislatures of the States concerned as well as of the Congress.

The Congress shall have Power to dispose of and make all needful Rules and Regulations respecting the Territory or other Property belonging to the United States; and nothing in this Constitution shall be so construed as to Prejudice any Claims of the United States, or of any particular State.

Section. 4.   The United States shall guarantee to every State in this Union a Republican Form of Government, and shall protect each of them against Invasion; and on Application of the Legislature, or of the Executive (when the Legislature cannot be convened) against domestic Violence.

ARTICLE. V.

The Congress, whenever two thirds of both Houses shall deem it necessary, shall propose Amendments to this Constitution, or, on the Application of the Legislatures of two thirds of the several States, shall call a Convention for proposing Amendments, which, in either Case, shall be valid to all Intents and Purposes, as Part of this Constitution, when ratified by the Legislatures of three fourths of the several States, or by Conventions in three fourths thereof, as the one or the other Mode of Ratification may be proposed by the Congress; Provided that no Amendment which may be made prior to the Year One thousand eight hundred and eight shall in any Manner affect the first and fourth Clauses in the Ninth Section of the first Article; and that no State, without its Consent, shall be deprived of its equal Suffrage in the Senate.

ARTICLE. VI.

All Debts contracted and Engagements entered into, before the Adoption of this Constitution, shall be as valid against the United States under this Constitution, as under the Confederation.

This Constitution, and the Laws of the United States which shall be

The Constitution of the United States

made in Pursuance thereof; and all Treaties made, or which shall be made, under the Authority of the United States, shall be the supreme Law of the Land; and the Judges in every State shall be bound thereby, any Thing in the Constitution or Laws of any State to the Contrary notwithstanding.

The Senators and Representatives before mentioned, and the Members of the several State Legislatures, and all executive and judicial Officers, both of the United States and of the several States, shall be bound by Oath or Affirmation, to support this Constitution; but no religious Test shall ever be required as a Qualification to any Office or public Trust under the United States.

ARTICLE. VII.

The Ratification of the Conventions of nine States, shall be sufficient for the Establishment of this Constitution between the States so ratifying the Same.

done in Convention by the Unanimous Consent of the States present the Seventeenth Day of September in the Year of our Lord one thousand seven hundred and Eighty seven and of the Independence of the United States of America the Twelfth In witness whereof We have hereunto subscribed our Names,
G̲O̲ WASHINGTON—Presid.t
   and deputy from Virginia

[Other signatures omitted]

Appendix

BILL OF RIGHTS

Amendment I

Congress shall make no law respecting an establishment of religion, or prohibiting the free exercise thereof; or abridging the freedom of speech, or of the press; or the right of the people peaceably to assemble, and to petition the Government for a redress of grievances.

Amendment II

A well regulated Militia, being necessary to the security of a free State, the right of the people to keep and bear Arms shall not be infringed.

Amendment III

No Soldier shall, in time of peace, be quartered in any house, without the consent of the Owner, nor in time of war, but in a manner to be prescribed by law.

Amendment IV

The right of the people to be secure in their persons, houses, papers, and effects, against unreasonable searches and seizures, shall not be violated, and no Warrants shall issue, but upon probable cause, supported by Oath or affirmation, and particularly describing the place to be searched, and the persons or things to be seized.

Amendment V

No person shall be held to answer for a capital or otherwise infamous crime, unless on a presentment or indictment of a Grand Jury, except in cases arising in the land or naval forces, or in the Militia, when in actual service in time of War or public danger; nor shall any person be subject for the same offence to be twice put in jeopardy of life or limb; nor shall be compelled in any criminal case to be a witness against himself, nor be

The first ten amendments were passed by Congress September 25, 1789. They were ratified by three-fourths of the states December 15, 1791.

deprived of life, liberty, or property, without due process of law; nor shall private property be taken for public use, without just compensation.

AMENDMENT VI

In all criminal prosecutions, the accused shall enjoy the right to a speedy and public trial, by an impartial jury of the State and district wherein the crime shall have been committed, which district shall have been previously ascertained by law, and to be informed of the nature and cause of the accusation; to be confronted with the witnesses against him; to have compulsory process for obtaining witnesses in his favor, and to have the Assistance of Counsel for his defence.

AMENDMENT VII

In suits at common law, where the value in controversy shall exceed twenty dollars, the right of trial by jury shall be preserved, and no fact tried by a jury, shall be otherwise reexamined in any Court of the United States, than according to the rules of the common law.

AMENDMENT VIII

Excessive bail shall not be required, nor excessive fines imposed, nor cruel and unusual punishments inflicted.

AMENDMENT IX

The enumeration in the Constitution, of certain rights, shall not be construed to deny or disparage others retained by the people.

AMENDMENT X

The powers not delegated to the United States by the Constitution; nor prohibited by it to the States, are reserved to the States respectively, or to the people.

Bibliographical Note

To treat so large a subject as the Revolution and the Constitution in so few pages as I have done suggests an intellectual arrogance which I take this opportunity to disavow. I pretend to know well only a small portion of the period I have covered; for the rest I have relied heavily on the works of other historians who have spent more lifetimes on the subject than I or any other individual has available. I wish to name here a few of those works I have found most useful, together with some in which the reader will find an antidote for my own conscious and unconscious peculiarities of viewpoint.

The first, and in many ways the greatest, historian of the Revolutionary period was the Jacksonian Democrat, George Bancroft. Sooner or later anyone who wishes to know the Revolution must go to his *History of the United States* (10 vols., 1834-74). Though he was not always scrupulous in his use of quotations, though he wrote the extravagant prose of the nineteenth century, though he saw the hand of God operating in places where we would not detect it, he nevertheless did know the sources better than anyone has since, and he did address himself to the central question: How did the United States come into being as a nation dedicated to principles of liberty and equality?

Subsequent historians have not been able to answer this question as successfully as Bancroft did, but they have revised his answer at many points, and they have also asked and answered many related questions that Bancroft neglected. They have, for example, examined more closely the latent forces making for coherence in American life before the Revolutionary period. Michael Kraus, *Intercolonial Aspects of American Culture*

Bibliographical Note

on the Eve of the Revolution (1928), shows how colonial Americans were joined together in a variety of mundane ways. The less tangible aspects of this coherence are discussed in Max Savelle, *Seeds of Liberty* (1948), and Clinton Rossiter, *Seedtime of the Republic* (1953), both of which emphasize the growth of ideas of liberty. Daniel J. Boorstin, in *The Americans: The Colonial Experience* (1958), probes the manifold ways in which a pragmatic approach to the problems of life distinguished the colonists from their Old World contemporaries. The first volume of Irving Brant's great life of Madison (*James Madison: The Virginia Revolutionist* [1941]) argues convincingly that Americans attained a high degree of nationality early in the Revolutionary dispute. And Richard Merritt, in *Symbols of American Community, 1735-1775* (1966), uses the techniques of content analysis to discover in colonial newspapers the signs of national consciousness among Americans before the Revolutionary struggle began.

Modern scholars have also done more justice to the virtues of the British Empire than Bancroft did. The works of George Louis Beer (*The Old Colonial System* [2 vols., 1912]; *Origins of the British Colonial System* [1908]; *British Colonial Policy, 1754-1765* [1907]) and of Charles McLean Andrews (*The Colonial Period of American History* [4 vols., 1934-38]) are outstanding in this respect. The latter's *Colonial Background of the American Revolution* (1924) is perhaps the wisest book yet written on the subject. A more inclusive study of the British Empire as a whole and of its history from mid-century to the Revolutionary period is Lawrence H. Gipson's monumental work, *The British Empire before the American Revolution* (15 vols., 1936-69). Professor Gipson contends that the British imperial system before the Revolution was designed for the benefit of all its members and not merely of the mother country. He presents this view more succinctly in *The Coming of the Revolution, 1763-1775* (1954). The internal structure of government within the thirteen colonies is best described in Leonard W. Labaree, *Royal Government in America* (1930).

Bancroft's celebration of colonial democracy has received new support from Robert R. Brown, *Middle-Class Democracy and the Revolution in Massachusetts, 1691-1780* (1955), and from Robert R. Brown and B. Katherine Brown, *Virginia, 1705-1786: Aristocracy or Democracy?* (1964). The Browns were the first to demonstrate that the majority of colonists in these two states enjoyed the right to vote. Their position is supported by a survey of voting in all the colonies in Chilton Williamson, *American Suffrage from Property to Democracy, 1760-1860* (1960). Other historians have traced the rising power of the legislative assemblies for whom the voters

Bibliographical Note

voted, notably Jack P. Greene, *The Quest for Power: The Lower Houses of Assembly in the Southern Royal Colonies, 1689-1776* (1963), and J. R. Pole, *Political Representation in England and the Origins of the American Republic* (1966).

The growth of colonial resistance to Great Britain is covered in a number of monographs. In *The Stamp Act Crisis: Prologue to Revolution* (1953) my wife and I have treated the beginnings of the development. In *The Navigation Acts and the American Revolution* (1951) Oliver M. Dickerson disclosed the important role played by the American Board of Customs Commissioners; and Thomas C. Barrow, *Trade and Empire: The British Customs Service in Colonial America, 1660-1775* (1967), emphasizes the ineffectiveness of the whole customs system. Bernard Bailyn has discussed the intellectual basis of colonial opposition to Parliamentary taxation in two major works, *The Origins of American Politics* (1968) and *The Ideological Origins of the American Revolution* (1967); and Pauline Maier has traced the rise of popular resistance to England in *From Resistance to Revolution* (1972). Two valuable accounts of particular episodes are Benjamin W. Labaree, *The Boston Tea Party* (1964), and Hiller B. Zobel, *The Boston Massacre* (1970).

Bancroft's view of British politics during the Revolutionary period has been outmoded by the studies of Sir Lewis Namier (*The Structure of Politics at the Accession of George III* [1929]; *England in the Age of the American Revolution* [1930]) and by a number of scholars influenced by Namier: Richard Pares, *King George III and the Politicians* (1953); Bernard Donoughue, *British Politics and the American Revolution: The Path to War, 1773-1775* (1965); John Brooke, *King George III* (1972); and P. D. G. Thomas, *British Politics and the Stamp Act Crisis: The First Phase of the American Revolution, 1763-1767* (1975). The Namier school has shown that no party system existed in this period, a view already advanced by Clarence Alvord in *The Mississipppi Valley in British Politics* (1916).

Alvord's work, though challenged in many particulars by Jack Sosin's *Whitehall and the Wilderness* (1961), is the classic one on the role of the West in the pre-Revolutionary crisis. I have touched this subject only lightly in the present volume, partly for lack of space, partly because I have not been persuaded that British treatment of the West before the Quebec Act bothered more than a small number of Americans. The role of the West after 1776 is covered in Thomas P. Abernethy, *Western Lands and the American Revolution* (1937), and in two articles by Merrill Jensen ("The Cession of the Old Northwest," *Mississippi Valley Historical Review*, XXIII,

Bibliographical Note

27; "The Creation of the National Domain," ibid., XXVI, 323). Julian Boyd's definitive edition of Jefferson's ordinance (*The Papers of Thomas Jefferson*, VI, 581) does much to clarify the origin and significance of that document, but should be read in conjunction with Robert F. Berkhofer, Jr., "Jefferson, the Ordinance of 1784, and the Origins of the American Territorial System," *William and Mary Quarterly*, 3d ser., XXIX, 231.

There are several studies of economic activity during the Revolutionary period. James F. Shepherd and Gary M. Walton's *Shipping, Maritime Trade, and the Economic Development of Colonial North America* (1972) is a quantitative analysis, focussed on the years 1768-72. Joseph A. Ernst's *Money and Politics in America 1755-1775* (1973) deals with British fiscal policy and its effect on the colonial economy. Robert A. East's *Business Enterprise in the American Revolutionary Era* (1938) surveys the subject in comprehensive fashion, but James B. Hedges' admirable study of a single firm, *The Browns of Providence Plantation* (1952), gives a more concrete picture and one that modifies some of East's conclusions.

The role of the British army in antagonizing the colonists during the years from 1763 to 1775 is decribed in John Shy, *Toward Lexington* (1965). Shy has also contributed some valuable insights into the social and political aspects of the ensuing war in *A People Numerous and Armed* (1976). Don Higginbotham's *The War of American Independence* (1971) gives a full account of the war, emphasizing these aspects. Piers Mackesy's *The War for America* (1964) tells the story from the British point of view. A more conventional but lively and readable narrative, devoted mainly to the war, is Page Smith's *A New Age Now Begins* (1976). The diplomatic side of the struggle is well told in Samuel F. Bemis, *The Diplomacy of the American Revolution* (1935), and Richard B. Morris, *The Peacemakers: The Great Powers and American Independence* (1965).

For an understanding of the Constitutional Convention and its work, there is no substitute for Madison's notes on the debates. These and the fragmentary notes of other members have been edited authoritatively in four volumes by Max Farrand (*Records of the Federal Convention of 1787* [1911-37]), but the reader may find more convenient the single-volume edition by Charles C. Tansill (*Documents Illustrative of the Formation of the Union of the American States* [1927]). The records of the various state ratifying conventions are contained in Jonathan Elliot's *Debates in the Several State Conventions* (5 vols., 1836), but a much larger collection of documents relating to the ratifying process is under way, edited by Merrill Jensen, et al., *The Documentary History of the Ratification of the*

Bibliographical Note

Constitution (1976–   ). Cecilia Kenyon has edited a convenient selection of Antifederalist arguments, with an important introduction, in *The Antifederalists* (1966).

The political results of the Revolution in the various states are discussed most comprehensively in Allan Nevins, *The American States during and after the Revolution* (1924), and in Jackson T. Main, *The Sovereign States, 1775–1783* (1973). Main analyzes the social composition of the upper houses in the new state legislatures in *The Upper House in Revolutionary America, 1763–1788* (1967), and he examines political divisions in several states during the Revolutionary period in *Political Parties before the Constitution* (1974). A similar analysis of divisions at the national level is Herbert J. Henderson's *Party Politics in the Continental Congress* (1974), which demonstrates the increasingly sectional alignment of votes. In *Men in Rebellion: Higher Governmental Leaders and the Coming of the American Revolution* (1973) James K. Martin compares the social and economic backgrounds of political leaders before and after the Revolution.

Social and economic divisions among the Revolutionists, reflected in their political divisions, have long been a subject of scholarly interest. One of the earliest works to stress such conflicts and to identify them as class conflicts was Carl Becker's study of the origins of the Revolution in New York, *History of Political Parties in the Province of New York, 1760–1776* (1909). Here Becker made his famous statement, repeated in many subsequent accounts of the period, that he was examining a contest not merely about home rule but also about who should rule at home. Arthur M. Schlesinger's *Colonial Merchants and the American Revolution* (1918) extended Becker's thesis throughout the colonies in a thoroughly documented study of the role played by the merchants prior to the Declaration of Independence. J. Franklin Jameson elaborated the concept in an influential series of lectures published under the title *The American Revolution Considered as a Social Movement* (1926). Jameson dealt with every type of social change, but his book helped to focus attention on the internal conflicts that accompany such change.

The same stress on economic and social divisions is found, though not to the same degree, in the works of Carl Bridenbaugh, whose definitive studies of colonial cities (*Cities in the Wilderness* [1938] and *Cities in Revolt* [1955]) have enlarged our understanding of the urban aspect of colonial social development far beyond what we know about other aspects. It was naturally in the cities, where land could not be widely owned, that class conflict was most acute.

Bibliographical Note

But the work that did more than any other to emphasize class conflict is Charles Beard's *Economic Interpretation of the Constitution* (1913). Although directed toward the contest over the drafting and ratification of the Constitution, the book pointed backward toward the Revolutionary years, with an implication that the Constitution was the successful culmination of a struggle by the rich and well-born to gain control of American society. The implication was made explicit in the works of Merrill Jensen (*The Articles of Confederation* [1940], *The New Nation* [1950], and *The American Revolution within America* [1974], where the Articles of Confederation are interpreted as an embodiment of the democratic philosophy of the Declaration of Independence and as hateful to the aristocratic elements for that reason.

In this view of things, the Revolution became the work of a group of radical democrats opposed by conservative aristocrats. Many of the aristocrats became loyalists in 1776, but others rode out the storm and eventually triumphed in a Thermidorean reaction with the adoption of the Constitution.

Such an interpretation of the Revolution and the Constitution has been challenged, not only in the present volume but in many others that have since appeared. Robert Brown in *Charles Beard and the Constitution* (1956) and Forrest McDonald in *We the People* (1958) demonstrated conclusively that Beard misinterpreted and misunderstood the evidence in his analysis of the economic interests of the members of the Constitutional Convention. Jackson Turner Main in *The Social Structure of Revolutionary America* (1965) disclosed a pattern of social mobility so fluid as to render meaningless any interpretation of the period resting on class conflict. Wallace Brown in *The King's Friends* (1965) showed that the loyalists were not aristocrats but represented a cross-section of the colonial population. Other recent studies of the loyalists (notably Mary Beth Norton, *The British-Americans: The Loyalist Exiles in England, 1774–1789* [1972], and Robert M. Calhoun, *The Loyalists in Revolutionary America, 1760–1781* [1973]) stress their general agreement with the views of other colonists before 1774 and their estrangement thereafter as the Revolutionary movement widened the aims and aspirations of Americans.

While the old emphasis on class conflict has disappeared from most studies of the Revolution, a fresh interest has appeared in the role of the poor and the dispossessed, notably in Staughton Lynd, *Slavery, Class Conflict, and the United States Constitution* (1967), and Jesse Lemisch, "The American Revolution seen from the Bottom Up," in B. J. Bernstein,

189

Bibliographical Note

ed., *Toward a New Past* (1968). Benjamin Quarles has disclosed the wide military participation of blacks in *The Negro in the American Revolution* (1961); Arthur Zilversmit describes the impact of the Revolution on the status of blacks in the northern states in *The First Emancipation* (1967); and Donald Robinson probes the political consensus that supported the continued existence of slavery in *Slavery in the Structure of American Politics, 1765–1820* (1971). My own explanation of the relationship of slavery to the development of American freedom is contained in *American Slavery, American Freedom: The Ordeal of Colonial Virginia* (1975).

Several studies have turned attention to the development of radical political ideas and activity. Gordon Wood's searching study of political thought in the period from 1776 to 1787, *The Creation of the American Republic* (1969), finds that Americans during these years were far more radical and democratic in their thinking than historians have generally supposed, but he shares some of Beard's suspicions of the founding fathers of the Constitution. Jackson Turner Main also portrays *The Antifederalists* (1961) as more radical than the Federalists. And several historians in Alfred Young, ed., *The American Revolution: Explorations in the History of American Radicalism* (1976), argue for the existence of a popular, lower-class ideology stressing economic and social goals. Thus the interpretation of the Revolution may be swinging back a little in Beard's direction.

It seems unlikely, however, that Beard can be revived, and the newer historians are not in fact attempting to revive him. Rather, they are seeking to measure more precisely the changes effected by the Revolution in American society. My assessment of those changes and of the continuing significance of the doctrine of equality stressed in *The Birth of the Republic* is contained in "Conflict and Consensus in the American Revolution," in Stephen G. Kurtz and James H. Hutson, eds., *Essays on the American Revolution* (1972), and in a collection of my own essays, *The Challenge of the American Revolution* (1976).

Important Dates

1763 Peace of Paris ends Seven Years War, February 10
      Grenville becomes Chancellor of the Exchequer, April

1764 Sugar Act passed, April 5
      Massachusetts, Rhode Island, Connecticut, New York, and
      Virginia protest

1765 Stamp Act passed, March 22
      Patrick Henry's Virginia Resolves passed, May 30
      Grenville falls; Rockingham ministry instituted, July
      Stamp Act Congress meets at New York, October 7-24

1766 Stamp Act repealed, March 18
      Declaratory Act passed, March 18
      Rockingham falls; ministry of William Pitt, Earl of Chatham,
      instituted, July

1767 Towshend Acts passed, June 26, 29, July 2
      Customs Commissioners arrive in Boston, November 5

1768 Lord Hillsborough becomes Secretary of State for the Colonies,
      January
      Massachusetts Circular Letter appears, February 11
      Riot over seizure of Hancock's sloop "Liberty," June 10
      Non-importation agreements made
      Massachusetts Convention meets, September 22
      British troops arrive at Boston, September 29

Important Dates

1769   Parliament revives statute of Henry VIII, February 9
Virginia Resolutions passed, May 16

1770   Ministry of Lord North begins, February
Boston Massacre, March 5
Townshend duties repealed except on tea, March
Non-importation collapses

1772   The "Gaspee" burned, June 10
Lord Dartmouth replaces Hillsborough as Secretary of State for the Colonies, August
Boston Committee of Correspondence begun, November 2

1773   Virginia sponsors intercolonial committees of correspondence, March 12
Tea Act passed, May 10
Boston Tea Party, December 16

1774   Coercive Acts passed: Boston Port Act, March 31; Massachusetts Government Act, May 20; Administration of Justice Act, May 20; Quartering Act, June 2
Quebec Act passed, June 22
First Continental Congress meets, September 5–October 27

1775   Battles of Lexington and Concord, April 19
Second Continental Congress assembles, May 10
Battle of Bunker Hill, June 17
Olive Branch Petition sent, July 8

1776   Congress recommends formation of new state governments, May 10–15
Resolution affirms independence, July 2
Declaration of Independence, July 4
Battle of Long Island, August 26
Battle of Trenton, December 26

1777   Howe enters Philadelphia, September 25
Burgoyne surrenders at Saratoga, October 17
Congress presents Articles of Confederation to the states, November 17

Important Dates

1778   Treaties with France concluded, February 6
France enters the war, June

1779   Spain enters the war, June

1780   Charleston, South Carolina, falls, May 12
Battle of Camden, August 16

1781   Virginia agrees to cede western land claims, January 2
Articles of Confederation proclaimed, March 1

1783   Peace treaty signed, September 3

1784   Jefferson's ordinance for the government of the West, April 23

1785   Ordinance passed for sale of western lands, May 20

1786   Annapolis Convention meets, September 11–14
Shays' Rebellion

1787   Constitutional Convention meets, May 25–September 17
Northwest Ordinance passed, July 13
Delaware ratifies the Constitution, December 7
Pennsylvania ratifies, December 12
New Jersey ratifies, December 18

1788   Georgia ratifies, January 2
Connecticut ratifies, January 9
Massachusetts ratifies, February 6
Maryland ratifies, April 28
South Carolina ratifies, May 23
New Hampshire ratifies, June 21
Virginia ratifies, June 26
New York ratifies, July 26

1789   North Carolina ratifies, November 21

1790   Rhode Island ratifies, May 29

Index

Index

Boston Massacre, 46–47, 49, 52
Boston Tea Party, 58
Botetourt, Governor, 48
Bowman, Thaddeus, 1
Braintree, Mass., 63
Breed's Hill, 69
British Empire, 8–11
Brown, John, 53
Bunker Hill, Battle of, 69, 77
Burgh, James, 74
Burgoyne, General John, 81
Burke, Edmund, 51
Burke, Thomas, 105
Butler, Pierce, 133

Calvinism, 6–7
Camden, S.C., battle at, 85
Canada: in British Empire, 8; administration of, 14, 59; French in, 43; expedition to, 77–78; expedition from, 81; and French alliance, 83; and peace negotiations, 86
Castle William, 39
Charles I, 63
Charleston, S.C., 7, 85
Church, disestablishment of, 96–97
Class conflict: and Revolution, 98–99; and Constitutional Convention, 130–33; and ratification of Constitution, 147–48. *See also* Equality
Clinton, General Henry, 84–85
Clymer, George, 149
Coercive Acts, 58–59, 62, 64, 68
Colonists: divisiveness of, 4–5; and the empire, 4–13; Protestantism of, 6–7; sincerity of, 50–52. *See also under names of individual colonies*
Committees of Correspondence,

55–57, 59–60
Common Sense, 71–75
Concord, Battle of, 2, 68, 77
Connecticut: and Stamp Act, 26; uses charter as constitution, 89; and slave trade, 95; retains established church, 97; and western lands, 107; ratifies Constitution, 150
Constitution: drafting of, 128–43; method of ratifying, 142, 149; objections to, 144–48; ratification of, 144–55; text of, 171–81
Constitutional Convention, 128–43; members of, 129–33; compromises in, 133; general agreement among members, 134–37; "Great Compromise" in, 137–41; and slavery, 139–41
Continental Army, 68, 107
Continental Congress: first, 60, 61–62, 64–66; second, 68; advises formation of independent state governments, 88; acts against slave trade, 95; lack of power to tax, 97–98, 104; and drafting of Articles of Confederation, 103–7; and paper money, 104–5; and western lands, 107–9
Cornwallis, Lord, 85–86
Currency, inflation of, 97–98, 104–5, 126–27
Customs Commissioners, American Borad of: created, 34; and "customs racketeering," 34–40; and Boston Massacre, 46–47; and "Gaspee" incident, 52–53

Dartmouth, Earl of, 67
Declaration of Independence, 75–76; purpose of, 82; and Ameri-

196

Index

Index

cles of Confederation, 107; and western lands, 107; Shays' Rebellion in, 126–27; opposition to Constitution in, 147–48; ratifies Constitution, 151–52

Massachusetts Circular Letter, 40–41, 49

Mercenaries, 70

Merchants: and non-importation agreements, 20, 48–49; and "customs racketeering," 36–40; pay taxes on tea and molasses, 50; and Tea Act, 57–58; and Revolutionary War, 97; in Confederation period, 117–19

Militia, 1–3, 68–69, 77, 79

Minute-men, 68

Mississippi Valley. See West

Mobs: in Boston, 20–21, 39, 45, 46–47, 54, 58; in Philadelphia, 150

Molasses, duty on, 10, 15, 36, 50

Molasses Act of 1733, 10

Montesquieu, 146–47

Morris, Gouverneur, 130, 139

Morris, Robert, 122, 123, 124

National bank, first, 123

Nationalism, 100–3. See also Americans, unity of

Natural rights, 73–75. See also Equality

Navigation Acts, 9–10, 26, 35–36, 117

New Hampshire, 6; retains established church, 97; and Articles of Confederation, 107; and New York, 116; ratifies Constitution, 153

New Jersey: royal governor of, 42; retreat across, 80; and Articles of Confederation, 107, 108; at Annapolis Convention, 128, 129; ratifies Constitution, 153

New Orleans, La., 121

Newport, R. I., 4, 7, 85

New York, 5, 7; and Sugar Act, 17–18; non-importation in, 20, 49; and billeting act, 32, 34, 35; and Quebec Act, 59; British in, 79, 81; and New Hampshire, 116; and federal impost, 125; at Annapolis Convention, 128–29; opposition to Constitution in, 147; Congress sits at, 149; ratifies Constitution, 153

Non-importation agreements: against Stamp Act, 20, 30; against Townshend duties, 34; ended, 49; and American character, 119

North, Lord: becomes Chancellor of Exchequer, 40; as first minister, 49; on equality, 66; conciliatory proposal by, 67; tries to resign, 86

North Carolina, 4, 6; and slavery, 95; and western lands, 107, 115–16; ratifies Constitution, 154–55

Northwest posts, 121

Northwest territory, 112–15. See also West

Nova Scotia, 59

Ohio Company, 113–15

Old Whigs, 29

Olive Branch Petition, 69, 70–71

Oliver, Andrew, 20–21

Otis, James, 5, 18, 24

Paine, Thomas, 6, 71–75

Parker, Captain John, 2

199

Index

Parliament: passes Navigation Acts, 9; position of, in English government, 11-13, 69-70; authority of, 15-19, 22-27, 34-35, 42-44, 48-49, 62-68; revives statute of Henry VIII, 47-48; passes Coercive Acts, 58-59; passes Quebec Act, 59; passes conciliatory resolve, 67; passes restraining act, 68; passes prohibitory act, 71

Paterson, William, 137

Paterson plan, 137

Pawtuxet, R. I., 53

Peace treaty, 86, 121

Pendleton, Edmund, 153

Pennsylvania: representation in, 24, 92; and Quebec Act, 59; abolishes office of governor, 91; adopts unicameral legislature, 92; at Annapolis Convention, 129; ratifies Constitution, 149-50

Philadelphia, 7; Continental Congress in, 61; Thomas Paine in, 71; British in, 81; Constitutional Convention in, 129

Pinckney, Charles, 134

Pitcairn, Major Thomas, 2

Pitt, William, 40; and repeal of Stamp Act, 28-29; on distinction between taxation and legislation, 29, 42, 67; and Declaratory Act, 31; becomes first minister, 32-33; becomes Lord Chatham. 33

Preston, Captain Robert, 47

Primogeniture, 98

Proclamation of rebellion, 71

Property: wide distribution of, 7, 72-74, 92-94, 97-99; and suffrage, 7, 92-93; and representation, 16-17; need for protection of, 126-27; and Constitutional Convention, 130-33, 141-42.

See also Representation; Taxation

Providence, R. I., 4, 53

Quebec Act, 59, 117

Rall, Colonel J. G., 81

Randolph, Edmund, 136, 137, 153

Randolph plan, 137-38

Religion, 6, 96-97

Representation: in colonial assemblies, 7; and taxation, 16-17, 23-27; of America in Parliament, 18-19, 23-24; in Massachusetts, 44-45; in state governments, 92-94; in national government, 137-39, 145-47. *See also* Virtual representation

Revere, Paul, 1

Rhode Island, 4; and ''Gaspee'' incident, 52-53; uses charter as constitution, 89; abolishes slave trade, 95; rejects federal impost, 124; and paper money, 126; and Constitutional Convention, 129; ratifies Constitution, 153-54

Rochambeau, Comte de, 84

Rockingham, Marquis of, 29-32

Rutledge, John, 61

Salaries: of governors and judges, 53-54; of congressmen, 132

Saratoga, N. Y., 82

Savannah, Ga., 85

Scotch-Irish, 5

Secretariat of State for Colonies, 40, 67

Secretary at War, 123

Secretary for Foreign Affairs, 123

Secretary of State for Southern

Index

Index

Virginia: resolves against Stamp
Act, 22–24, 26; resolves of 1769,
48; and Committees of Correspondence, 57; and Quebec Act,
59; proposes independence, 75;
campaign in, 85; state constitution of, 90; bill of rights in, 91;
and slavery, 95; permits manumission of slaves, 96; effect of
war on, 97; and western lands,
107–11; and Kentucky, 116; and
Annapolis Convention, 128–29;
and Constitutional Convention,
129; ratifies Constitution, 152–
53

Virtual representation: upheld, 18–
19; attacked, 23–24, 62, 70

Voting, 7, 92–93. *See also* Property

Walpole, Sir Robert, 14

Warren, Joseph, 101

Washington, George, 122, 153;
commands Continental Army,
68–69; forces evacuation of
Boston, 77; and Battle of Long
Island, 80; crosses and recrosses
Delaware, 80–81; retreats across
New Jersey, 80; loses Philadelphia, 81; victory of, at Yorktown, 85–86; on importance of
national government, 125; at
Constitutional Convention, 129,
146

Washington County, N.C., 115

Watauga Association, 115

West: British administration of, 14,
59, 116–17; representation of, in
state governments, 92–93; and
Articles of Confederation, 107–
17; and ordinance of 1784, 113;
and ordinance of 1785, 113–14;
and ordinance of 1787, 114–16;
and proposed treaty with Spain,
121–22; in Constitutional Convention, 138–39

West Indies, 8, 10, 84

Whately, Thomas, 18–19, 23

William of Orange, 16

Wilson, James, 64, 125–26, 138

Wythe, George, 153

Yorktown, Va., 85–86